Meditations for

MW00674440

Timeouts
with
God

 By Rochelle Melander and Harold Eppley

CPH
SAINT LOUIS

For Sam—
who is always willing
to save space for us
on the "timeout" chair.

Scripture notations marked NRSV are from the New Revised Standard Version of the Bible, copyright ©1989. Used by permission.

All Scripture quotations, unless otherwise indicated, are taken from the HOLY BIBLE, NEW INTERNATIONAL VERSION©. NIV®. Copyright © 1973, 1978, 1984 by International Bible Society. Used by permission of Zondervan Publishing House. All rights reserved.

Scripture notations marked CEV are from the CONTEMPORARY ENGLISH VERSION of the Bible. Copyright © American Bible Society, 1995. Used by permission.

Copyright © 2000 Rochelle Melander and Harold Eppley
Concordia Publishing House
3558 S. Jefferson Avenue, St. Louis, MO 63118-3968
Manufactured in the United States of America

Library of Congress Cataloging-in-Publication Data
Melander, Rochelle.
    Timeouts with God : meditations for parents / by Rochelle Melander and Harold Eppley.
        p. cm.
        ISBN 0-570-05276-9
        1. Parents—Prayer-books and devotions—English.
    2. Parenting—Religious aspects—Christianity—Meditations.
    I. Eppley, Harold. II. Title.
        BV4845 .M45 2001
        242'.645—dc21   00-011889

1 2 3 4 5 6 7 8 9 10   00 09 08 07 06 05 04 03 02 01

Acknowledgments

This book exists because the good people at CPH believe busy parents need to take "timeout" for God. We thank Rachel Hoyer, who received our proposal with great enthusiasm, and Dawn Weinstock for her support and wise editorial guidance.

We thank those people who helped us care for our son Sam while we wrote: the wonderful teachers at Premiere Ecole preschool, Jonathan Breimeier and the Monday "buddies," the Veseth-Rogers family, and our parents.

We thank the colleagues, parishioners, and friends who encouraged us to keep writing, especially Peter Rogness and the members of Nativity Lutheran Church.

And, of course, we thank God—who called us together through writing and who now calls us to write together. Writing this book has been part of our daily devotion. When we write, we do so to praise God, who gives us both our gifts and the desire to use them fruitfully. Thanks be to God!

Introduction

If your life as a parent looks anything like ours, you're busy. You juggle a variety of tasks and roles related to raising your family, maintaining your home, and earning a living. When you take time to read and study the Bible, you may discover a world that at first glance appears quite different from the one you live in. You may struggle to understand how the story of Jesus relates to your daily life as a parent in the 21st century.

The gospel story (and, in fact, the whole Bible) is not simply an ancient yarn, but the narrative of a living God. The same Jesus who walked beside the Sea of Galilee and called out to His first disciples also speaks to us. Each day our risen Savior tugs at our hearts and invites us to follow Him. Jesus promises to shower us with His abundant blessings. Jesus calls us to serve as lights for the Kingdom of God, both within our families and in the world.

Last summer, despite a busy schedule and a busier pre-school-age son, we added daily morning prayer to our schedule. We chose a devotional guide and set aside six weeks to complete the course. Every day, we listened to music, prayed together, read the Bible, and discussed the devotion. Then we each took time to record some of our prayer concerns in a personal journal.

During that six-week period, our lives did not slow down. We did. By taking timeout, we were able to approach each day with a renewed sense of our Savior's constant presence and guidance in our lives. We saw many of God's blessings we had previously been missing simply because we had failed to pay attention to them.

We hope this book of devotions will nudge your shoulder, tug at your heart, and remind you to take "timeout" from being a caretaker and wage-earner, to focus on your most important role—living as a baptized and redeemed child of God. Each devotion provides a connection between God's living Word and your daily life as a Christian parent.

As you read *Timeouts with God*, you might choose to keep a devotional journal. In it you can record meaningful Bible passages, ideas about how God's Word relates to your life, and prayers for your family and friends. You may reflect upon these devotions alone, with your spouse, or with another parent.

We pray this book will encourage you as a parent by reminding you of your Savior's unfailing love for your family. We hope your "timeout with God" will help you to pay closer attention to the many blessings Christ showers upon you every day.

In Jesus' name,

Rochelle and Harold

Timeout with God

Luke 5:15–16; Matthew 6:5–6

At our house, whenever our son misbehaves, we tell him he must take a "timeout." That means he sits on a chair by himself until he has sufficiently pondered his misbehavior and decides to say he's sorry.

This is the most common form of "timeout" in our house. But we also use it another way. Sometimes, as a preschooler, our son experiences moments when he becomes overexcited and overwhelmed by his life's daily events. He works himself into a frantic pace, chattering and rushing from one activity to another, resembling a tornado more than a toddler. We are tempted to post signs alerting visitors to our home to the danger: *Warning: 4-year-old has reached gale-force velocity—can wreak destruction upon entire room in less than 10 seconds!*

"Timeout!" we shout. But unlike those times when he's misbehaving, Sam responds to us immediately. In these moments, he seems to realize that his life has become too frenzied. He understands he needs to slow down, take a break, and allow calmness to return to his stormy life.

As parents, we also often find ourselves living at a breakneck pace. We scurry about, clutching our never-ending "to do" lists as we race to meet deadlines both at work and at home. We know we are not alone. Many parents complain that their daily routine involves constantly rushing from one activity to another. In stressful moments, we often say we need more time. In fact, what we need is more "timeout." We need timeout with God to pray, study Scripture, and examine our lives from God's perspective.

In Jesus' busy days of ministering on this earth, He frequently took "timeout" to pray to and be alone with His heavenly Father. If we think our lives are stressful, imagine what

Jesus' daily routine was like. He spent hours preaching, teaching, and working miracles while surrounded by thousands of people who were full of questions and in need of much attention. Jesus also faced the stress of knowing His life was leading to Calvary's cross.

Jesus is the very Son of God, with power beyond our imagination. Yet Jesus made a regular practice of retreating from His hectic schedule to quietly focus upon what He had come to do. If Jesus took "timeout," shouldn't we follow His example?

Martin Luther said whenever the devil tempted him into thinking he did not have time to pray, he would pray all the longer. We also might be tempted to think we are too busy to take timeout with God. If we are rushing around taking care of our children, making meals, cleaning our homes, and heading off to our jobs, we need to stop and ask ourselves some serious questions. Who gave us the ability to work? Who blesses us with the gifts of home, family, and daily bread? Who gives us life, and even more important, eternal life?

If you are a parent, you don't need more time. You need more "timeout" with Jesus.

Dear Jesus,

just as You took "timeout" to pray
and gather strength for Your ministry
on this earth, remind me that I need to do
the same. When I start to rush from task to task,
reach out to me, slow me down,
and help me to see my life
from Your perspective.

Amen.

Faith Journey

Hebrews 11:1–3, 8–12

Have you ever taken off on a journey, knowing where you were headed, but not quite sure how you would get there? Chances are, you got lost somewhere along the way. We remember one of our first trips together, when we ventured through the great city of Chicago without a map.

Both of us grew up in small towns where getting lost was no big deal. Getting lost on the Chicago tollway is a different story. We were driving in bumper-to-bumper traffic, moving at 70 miles per hour in the left-most lane of an eight-lane highway, when we saw the sign informing us that the exit we wanted was in the right-most lane and it was coming up in one-eighth of a mile. As you might guess, we missed the exit. We drove on, lost in the big city, many miles from home. If you've ever been lost, then you know it can be a dreadful, frightening feeling.

The letter to the Hebrews reminds us that all Christians, even those who don't venture out much, are traveling on a journey. It is a faith journey, in which we know where we're headed (heaven!), but we're not sure what twists and turns lie ahead. The writer of Hebrews compares our Christian faith journey to the one Abraham and Sarah made many years ago: "By faith Abraham, when called to go to a place he would later receive as his inheritance, obeyed and went, even though he did not know where he was going" (Hebrews 11:8).

We too travel by faith. We know that through the death and resurrection of our Savior Jesus Christ, God has promised to bring us one day into the glory of everlasting life. God has also promised to guide us as we journey through this life on our way to heaven. That doesn't mean the journey will always be easy.

Sometimes our human sinfulness causes us to become too self-reliant. We neglect to consult our map (God's Word). We lose contact with our Navigator. We get lost along the way.

Occasionally, even when we do follow God's Word, God leads us in directions we would rather not go. We may encounter a few detours, potholes, and hairpin curves along the way. Our path will take us through the dark valley of the shadow of death—for all roads must pass that way. In our sinfulness, we may sometimes lose faith in our Navigator. We may start to doubt that the road we're taking leads to the glorious destination Christ has promised. None of us remains ever faithful to God. Yet even if we lose confidence in His guidance, our Savior never stops leading us. Christ never leaves us lost and alone.

Parenting is also a faith journey. Becoming a parent is like choosing a scenic route over the expressway—it usually takes longer to get where you're going. Yet if you pay attention, you will discover wonders you would have never known existed had you taken the faster route. Take time to enjoy the blessings along the road of parenting. And rest assured that when the journey is done, your Navigator will lead you safely home.

Jesus,

You are my Navigator.
I do not know what lies ahead for me today.
Grant me the confidence to trust
in Your guidance.

Amen.

Just Like Dad

1 Corinthians 4:14–17; 11:1–2

"Sam! What on earth do you think you're doing?!"

Rochelle had caught our son in the middle of an act that is strictly forbidden at our house. As she placed food on the supper table, she turned to see him stick his finger into the serving bowl of mashed potatoes. With the evidence of his crime on his hands and face, Sam turned to the best option for making his defense.

"But Daddy does it," he pleaded.

Suddenly two male members of the family were in trouble.

"Harold, is this true?" asked Rochelle. "Do you stick your fingers in the serving bowls?"

Now Harold couldn't very well lie about this, could he? "Well ... uh ... maybe I did it once or twice," he admitted. "But I didn't realize Sam was watching me."

Our children are *always* watching us. We are fooling ourselves if we think they aren't. Children learn by imitation, by copying the actions and habits of others. Even as infants, children carefully observe parents and other family members and then mirror their behavior. If you are the parent of a preschooler, you may be quite aware of the influence you exert on your children. You have probably heard your child say he or she wants to be "just like mom or dad."

If you are the parent of a teenager, you may be longing for the "good ol' days" when your son or daughter reveled in following your example. It may seem the teen in your house always tries to be exactly the opposite of you (just to annoy you, of course). But don't fool yourself—your child is still watching you. Your teenagers look to you as an example even if they refuse to acknowledge your influence.

Sometimes, as parents, we tell our children, "Do as I say not as I do." This is *not* a Scriptural approach to parenting. John wrote, "Dear children, let us not love with words or tongue but with actions and in truth" (1 John 3:18). Paul often encouraged his readers to imitate his behavior: "Follow my example, as I follow the example of Christ" (1 Corinthians 11:1).

As Christian parents, God calls us to be role models for our children. We can hardly expect our children to make Christ their top priority if we do not do the same. Actions really do speak louder than words. Although we know our children will learn and grow in their faith as they attend worship and Sunday school, they will most consistently learn how to live out their faith in the home. As parents, we are the most important influence in their lives.

Of course, none of us is perfect. On occasion, even the best of us get caught with our fingers in the mashed potatoes. When our children see our mistakes (and gleefully point them out to us), it is important that we acknowledge our shortcomings. We can positively influence our children's faith by reminding them "that all have sinned" and cannot be saved except by the gracious mercy of our Lord Jesus Christ. Again, Paul serves as a helpful model. Though he told his readers to follow his example, Paul openly acknowledged his own imperfections (see Romans 7:21–25) and his need for Jesus Christ.

Our children are watching us closer than most of us realize. May all our words and actions, both our accomplishments and our mistakes, point them to the most important role model of all. May our children learn to look to Christ, who loves us even when we fail to follow His example.

Prayer idea: Ask Christ to make you more aware of the influence you have upon your children and help you to become a better example for them.

Growing Pains

Ephesians 4:14–16

"My, how he's grown since I last saw him."

Most parents hear comments like this so often that they almost sound like clichés. At extended family gatherings or visits with friends we see occasionally, we know we can always count on somebody to remark about our son's most recent growth spurt.

Growth, obviously, is good, given that the alternatives are stagnancy and death. Thus, it is no wonder the Bible speaks about our need to grow in the Christian faith. God's grace working within us produces growth. Plants need gifts from their Creator, water and sunshine, to thrive in this world. We, too, rely on our Creator for the nourishment needed to grow. Without the waters of Baptism and daily doses of our Savior's Sonshine, we would wither and decay.

Like many Christian parents, we pray that as our son grows in years, he will also grow in faith in God and love toward others. We also say this prayer for ourselves. Sometimes when we pray for spiritual growth, we forget that the process of growing is not always easy. In fact, growth can be quite painful.

Our human bondage to sin often causes us to resist growth and remain stagnant in our faith. Parents know that the transition from infancy to adulthood is no easy task (although many days we wish it were). From toilet training to teenage tirades, parents encounter much resistance as they seek to help their children mature physically, socially, and emotionally.

One day, when our son was in the midst of his "terrible 2s," a friend looked at Rochelle and said, "You don't look good."

"I'm suffering from growing pains—not mine, but Sam's," she replied.

We imagine that it hurts God to watch us struggling to grow in our faith. It must seem like a spiritual tug-of-war as our Savior seeks to teach us His ways and we resist like stubborn 2-year-olds. What joy God must feel when we finally do make strides, when the love of Christ propels us forward and we move closer to becoming all God wants us to be.

Growing is neither quick nor easy. It is a constant process—a few steps forward, a few steps back. Yet as the Holy Spirit opens our hearts for Christ to have His way with us, to teach us and fill us with His grace, we grow in love for God and for others. Some days the growth will seem immeasurable. Eventually we will be able to reflect on our lives and say, "My, how I've grown. And Jesus deserves all the credit!"

Thank You,
Lord God,

for the patience You have shown me
as I have struggled to grow in my faith.

Thank You for not giving up on me
in difficult times. Make me patient
with my own children in the midst
of their growing pains.

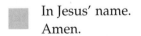 In Jesus' name.
Amen.

"God Said It Was Good"

Genesis 1:1–2:2

After church each Sunday, we walk home discussing the morning. Most weeks our son has few words to add to the conversation. He will often tell us what he had for a snack during Sunday school, especially if it was something he likes. He talks about who was there, "Kai, and Rachel, and Jacki, and Alex." Only rarely will he tell us about the lesson. One Sunday, Sam broke his silence. "So what did you talk about in Sunday school?" asked Rochelle.

"God said it was good." replied Sam.

"Oh," responded Rochelle. "Do you remember *what* God said was good?"

Silence.

"How about the light?"

Sam replied, "God said it was good."

Throughout the rest of the day, Sam repeated his lesson from Sunday school. As we read the newspaper, walked around the block, ate supper, and picked up toys, Sam reminded us, "God said it was good."

Sam became a bit of a prophet that day. If a prophet's job is to present people with the truth, to hold up a mirror to their lives and say, "Pay attention! Listen to what God has to say!"— then Sam was a prophet (albeit a gentle one). So often we go about our days complaining about trivial matters. We moan because we have too much to do, or the dinner was overcooked, or our children did not pick up their toys. We become overwhelmed by our daily tasks and grumble about how hard our lives seem to be. In the midst of our moaning and groaning and complaining, we lose sight of the gifts God has given to us. Sam's constant litany, "God said it was good," reminded us that our lives really are full of blessings.

In the first chapter of Genesis, we read about God creating the earth. The verse Sam was quoting actually says, "God saw that it was good" (Genesis 1:10). And that's just it. We look at our lives and complain because our sinfulness affects our ability to see clearly. God looks at our lives and He sees what is good. God sees beyond our sinfulness and the daily troubles that sometimes cloud our vision. God sees Christ within us (Colossians 1:27) and around us, blessing all our days.

Maybe we all need to spend the day saying, "God said it was good." It might help us see more of the countless ways God blesses us every moment we live.

Creator God,

You love us,
Your creations, more
deeply than we can imagine.
Grant us clearer vision
so we can see Your goodness
in all that we are
and all that we have.
In Jesus' name.

Amen.

Let There Be Light

Matthew 5:14–16

Rochelle sat in the church nursery, watching over 10 little ones while their parents attended the Thanksgiving Eve service. Becky, a teenager, tried to entertain three little girls with a story. Emily, Becky's big sister, held the lone baby on her hip and made cooing noises. Rochelle divided her time between the rest of the children, some crawling on the floor with toys, others quietly coloring pictures of Jesus.

Suddenly the lights went out. The nursery sunk into darkness. Children cried and screamed. Becky and Emily, knowing their 2-year-old brother Matt loved to play with the light switch, shouted, "Matt! Turn the lights on!" He did. The nursery was bathed in light once again. Little Joey, almost 4 years old, turned to Rochelle and said, "That darkness was not good at all. We need light."

Thank you, Joey. We need to hear that message again and again. The darkness is not good. We do need light. Jesus said, "I am the light of the world" (John 8:12). In the sermon on the mount, our Savior tells us that we too are lights in the world (Matthew 5:14). St. Paul reminds us that Christ's light has been placed within us: "For God who said, 'Let light shine out of darkness,' made His light shine in our hearts to give us the light of the knowledge of the glory of God in the face of Christ" (2 Corinthians 4:6).

As Christians, we reflect Christ's light. We are like the moon to the sun. We are not the source of the light, yet we can make a difference. If we don't let our light shine, the world will indeed be a darker place.

Unfortunately, we don't always allow our light to shine. Sometimes the darkness of our sins overshadows us and we fail to love others the way Christ loves us. Or we feel as though what we do doesn't really matter, so we pass over opportunities to share the message of Christ's incredible love with our children and our neighbors.

Yet no matter how often we fail, we continue to be lights in this world. Jesus didn't say that we *should* be lights. Or that we *could* be. Or that we *ought* to be. He simply said that we *are*. We are a light of the world, reflecting Christ who is *the* light. We do not cease to be parents simply because we sometimes neglect to act like responsible parents. Likewise, we do not stop being Christians just because we don't always live the way God wants us to.

A few years ago, on Christ the King Sunday, we sang a closing hymn that was the old vacation Bible school favorite, "This Little Light of Mine." Pastors and lay people, young and old, sang loudly, our hands held as high as we were able, promising God and one another that we would go out into the world with our lights aglow. In the end, this song says it all for us. God calls us to let our lights shine, reflecting the love our Savior has first sparked within us.

Lord Jesus,
> shine through me

> so others may see
> Your gift of salvation

> and
> praise our Father in heaven.

> Amen.

From My Mother's Womb

Psalm 22:9–11; Matthew 6:25–30

Once, before our son was born, both of us came down with the flu. Wrapped in quilts, we settled on the sofa for a day of television viewing (something our normal schedule never allowed us to do). We felt quite well mentally *until* we turned on the television. As we watched talk shows, news, and the accompanying commercials, we heard that we have much to fear.

The problems started with us: we weren't attractive enough, didn't wear the right clothes, or drive the safest car. We owned a hopelessly out-of-date computer. We didn't use the right deodorant, toothpaste, hand lotion, shampoo, and soap. On top of that, nearly everything in our house, especially the food, could (and probably would) cause cancer someday soon. Then there was all the scary stuff going on around the world and in our neighborhood that might happen to us next—robberies, car accidents, phone scams, and more. Before we became totally depressed, we turned off the television and turned on some soothing music.

We learned an important lesson that morning (besides the obvious, "don't watch too much television")—we live in an anxious world. In fact, we could spend our entire days just worrying about everything that *might* happen to us. Now that we are parents, the possibilities for worry seem to be endless. A simple trip to the doctor's office or a glance at the latest parenting magazine presents a whole new list of matters to worry about. We've come to the conclusion that we have to think about these lurking fears in a new way ... or we'll never survive parenting, let alone life.

A few verses from Psalm 22 have helped us. Like much of the Bible, these words remind us that God is in control of our lives. David wrote, "Yet You brought me out of the womb; You made me trust in You even at my mother's breast. From birth I was cast upon You; from my mother's womb You have been my God. Do not be far from me, for trouble is near and there is no one to help" (Psalm 22:9–11).

As parents, we will worry. Sometimes our concerns are legitimate. We humans cannot rely on ourselves or others to always do what is right or safe. Like David, we live in a world where "trouble is near."

Yet God has provided for us since we were within our mother's womb. If God could love us and watch over us even when we were yet unseen by the world, then God is clearly able to help us now. That doesn't mean we are immune from trouble. It does mean that as God's children, we can trust in His constant presence and power, especially when difficulties occur.

St. Paul wrote, "Do not be anxious about anything, but in everything, by prayer and petition, with thanksgiving, present your requests to God" (Philippians 4:6). God encourages us to share all our worries and concerns with Him. Then He goes on to make a promise those television commercials cannot make. God doesn't guarantee whiter teeth, a safer car, or a cure for cancer. God promises something better—His grace through Jesus Christ. "And the peace of God, which transcends all understanding, will guard your hearts and your minds in Christ Jesus" (Philippians 4:7).

O God,

sometimes I worry about my family and myself.
Remind me that You have protected
and guided me through life thus far
and You will always be my God
no matter what I face.
In Jesus' name.
Amen.

In a Hurry

Job 37:5–14

Harold's in a hurry. It's a four-block walk to the convenience store. At a brisk pace, he figures he should be able to get there, pick up what he needs, and arrive back home in 10 minutes. There's one major problem, however. Harold is not moving at a brisk pace. Three-year-old Sam is accompanying him on this walk. And Sam's in no hurry to get anywhere.

Harold is thinking about the many tasks to which he must attend before this day is over. The more he thinks, the faster he walks. Or tries to ... Sam keeps dawdling. "Look, Daddy, see that flower. I like that flower. It's a purple flower. Look, Daddy. A birdie. In the tree. See the tree, Daddy? A doggie, a doggie, a doggie! Can we pat the doggie, please?"

"Sam, we don't have time. We need to get supper on the table before your mother comes home. And I have a meeting tonight. Come on, Sam. Hurry up!"

Harold is practically dragging Sam behind him. Why didn't we take the car, he wonders. Getting Sam into the car is such an ordeal that sometimes it's quicker to walk. With Sam, everything moves slowly.

Harold glances at his watch. At this rate, he thinks, I'll never get to that meeting on time. ...

"What's this, Daddy?" Sam has stopped walking. He is peering down at the sidewalk, pointing at a caterpillar no larger than his thumb. The tiny creature slithers across the cement, apparently in no more of a hurry than Sam.

"Come on, Sam. We don't have time to waste."

Sam is squatting now, his head bent over, his face just inches from the sidewalk. He doesn't touch the caterpillar. He watches it with his eyes and mouth wide open. "He's crawling," says Sam. "I like him."

Harold has stopped. What else can he do? He clenches his jaw, puts his hands on his hips. He wants to yell. He wants to wave his fist in the air. More than anything, he wants this day to be over with. He is about to yell ... when suddenly something comes over him. He remembers a Bible passage, one he read a few days before, a verse from the book of Job: "stop and consider God's wonders" (Job 37:14).

Stop. There is no voice from heaven, no great epiphany. Just the memory of a Bible passage that the Holy Spirit has poured into Harold's heart at the moment when he needs it most.

Stop and consider God's wonders. The purple flower. The birdie. The tree. The doggie. The caterpillar. A curious little boy. Stop and consider. Life itself. Eternal life. And the greatest gift of all. Our Savior Jesus Christ.

Suddenly the meeting didn't seem so important. They could eat sandwiches for supper. Harold couldn't even remember why they were going to the store.

"It's a caterpillar, Sam. It's one of God's wonders. Know what else, Sam? You're one of God's wonders too."

"Daddy?"

"Yes, Sam."

"I like the cabberpillar. Can we take it home?"

Prayer idea:

STOP,
look around,
consider God's wonders,
and thank the One who made them all.

Keeping Track

If you are the parent of more than one child, you may have heard a few conversations like this one:

"Mom! Dad! Tommy hit me!"

"Did not!"

"Did too!"

"Well, you hit me first."

"Did not. I just tapped you. Besides you dropped my teddy bear in the toilet."

"That was an accident. You spilled lemonade on my baseball cards."

"You said you forgave me for that."

"Well, I didn't mean it."

"Mom! Dad!"

Keeping the peace in a family is no easy matter, partly because many children (and adults) like to keep track of all the times they have been wronged. When Peter asked Jesus how many times he should forgive those who sinned against him, Jesus answered, "I tell you, not seven times, but seventy-seven times" (Matthew 18:22).

Jesus didn't mean we should keep track of how many times we forgive others. He meant quite the opposite. Jesus wants our forgiveness to have no limits.

Jesus wants us to forgive one another without ceasing because that's how God forgives each of us. Time and again, we sin and fall short of God's standards. Whenever we come crawling back, begging for God's mercy, God forgives us all our wrongs. God doesn't keep track of all the times we've hurt Him. In fact, when we repent, God promises to forget our sins. God says, "I, even I, am He who blots out your transgressions, for My own sake, and remembers your sins no more" (Isaiah 43:25).

God has forgiven our every past wrong. God promises to forgive our every future sin. As we turn from our sin and receive His gracious mercy, God wants us to do the same for one another. That is the vow couples make when they are married. When they promise to love and keep each other "for better and for worse," they are promising to forgive each other for sins they have not yet committed. We make that same unspoken vow on the day our children are born. We promise to love them and forgive them no matter how much they might hurt us in the future.

Jesus' words also remind us that forgiveness is an ongoing process. Many times we forgive others and think we have recovered from the pain their actions caused us. Then suddenly, something happens to remind us of the pain. It is like reinjuring a wound that has not quite healed. Thus, we may find ourselves needing to forgive someone over and over for the same single offense.

Only with the Holy Spirit's help can any of us forgive. If we were to add up all the sins everyone has ever committed against us, they would be a mere pittance compared to the number of times we have sinned against God. When we ponder all Christ has first done for us, we start to realize that forgiving others is not too much for God to ask of us.

Our Father, who art in heaven ...

forgive us our trespasses as we forgive
those who trespass against us. In Jesus' name.
Amen.

No Need to Hide

Jeremiah 23:23–24

Around the age of 1 or 2, children pass through a stage in which they think they can make themselves disappear merely by closing their eyes. Since they cannot see anything, they mistakenly believe nobody else can see them. Most children quickly grow out of this stage. Soon they discover that no matter how hard they try, they can never make themselves invisible.

Still, children sometimes wish they could simply close their eyes and vanish. When mom screams, "Who broke the cookie jar?" they may scramble to the nearest closet, hoping their mother will not find them. When the teacher asks for the answers to the homework assignment they did not do, they may stare down at their desk and pray they will not be called upon.

Many adults caught in an act of impropriety have wished they could suddenly become invisible. Speeding motorists, catching a glimpse of flashing lights in the rear view mirror, might hope they could miraculously vaporize into thin air.

Of course, it all goes back to the beginning. The Bible tells us that after Adam and Eve had disobeyed God's command, they hid when they heard God walking in the garden (Genesis 3:8). We might think Adam and Eve were foolish to believe they could actually conceal themselves from God. Yet we behave in much the same way when we find ourselves in trouble. We fool ourselves into believing God cannot always see us.

There is a story about a pastor who stepped into a room where a number of his parishioners had been gossiping. As soon as they saw him, a hush fell over the room. "As you were," said the pastor. "If it's good enough for God to hear, it's good enough for me to hear."

The prophet Jeremiah wrote: " 'Can anyone hide in secret places so that I cannot see him?' declares the LORD" (3:24). We might fool our children, our spouses, or our friends. But we can't fool God. Before our Creator, we all stand visible. God sees all our sins, including those we are able to hide from other people. God even knows about the sins we conceal from ourselves.

God has seen it all. We know what God has done about it. God sent Jesus, the One without sin, to save us. And Jesus did not hide. In fact, He suffered and died on a cross, in a most visible place, for all the world to see.

As parents, we expect that our children will occasionally try to conceal their actions from us. No doubt, they will get away with a few of their "crimes," just as we did as children. Parents cannot see everything. Thankfully, neither we nor our children need to hide from the One who can see all. God sees us at our worst and still promises to comfort, embrace, and forgive us through Jesus.

Lord God,

> sometimes I fool myself into thinking
> I can hide my sins from You.
> Forgive me my foolishness
> and remind me that because of Christ,
> I do not need to hide from You.

> In my Savior's name, I pray.
> Amen.

Loving Yourself

Mark 12:28–31

A teacher of the law asked Jesus which commandment is the most important. Our Savior responded with two commands: "Love the LORD your God ... and love your neighbor as yourself" (Mark 27:30–31). *As yourself.* Jesus' words remind us that if we do not love ourselves well, we may find it difficult to love others.

We live in an age when it is trendy to talk about growing up in a dysfunctional family. Ideally, you were raised by loving parents. Still, many people do grow up in unhealthy family settings. Many children experience verbal, emotional, physical, or sexual abuse. When children experience such abuses, even mildly, they frequently have difficulty believing God loves them.

When we do not believe that God loves us, when we peer into our spiritual mirror and cringe at what we see, loving others becomes a challenge. Our self-hatred often turns outward to our nearest neighbors—our spouses and our children.

The first step in overcoming this self-hatred is letting God's whispers of love reach us. Many children who were abused struggle to accept the fact that God could find them lovable. They feel there must be a catch somewhere, that they need to *do* something to receive this most precious gift. In the Bible, God says to us: "you are precious in my sight, and honored, and I love you" (Isaiah 43:4a NRSV). Those who have felt unlovable for their entire lives or even just for a few moments need to hear the good news that God demonstrates His own love for us in this: "While we were still sinners, Christ died for us" (Romans 5:8).

Paul makes it clear that we do not need to *do* anything to receive God's grace through our Savior Jesus Christ. We only need to believe that Jesus' death and resurrection was "for us." Each time we hear the words "given for you" as we receive the bread and the wine at the Lord's Table, our Savior reminds us that His love is indeed *for us.*

As we hear Christ's whispers of love, He works in us and through us and we begin to believe we are God's beautiful creation, "fearfully and wonderfully made" (Psalm 139:14). When we live in the knowledge of being wonderfully created by God and grow in our understanding of what it means to be loved, we begin to love ourselves. We may take baby steps at first. We may still have trouble looking in the mirror and seeing that we are lovable. But day by day, as we lean on God and bask in Christ's love, as we feel the strength and courage that comes from being unconditionally accepted by God, we will begin to love ourselves.

We will peek in the mirror and see that through our Savior's death and resurrection, God has made us beautiful. We will look at our lives and see the many ways God has gifted us. And from that place, we will be better able to love our neighbors. We will embrace our spouses and our children with a new confidence ... the assurance that comes only from knowing we are loved and redeemed by God.

Loving God,

You created me
and have known me from the beginning.
I thank You for Your unconditional love.
Grant me the confidence to depend on that love
and to share it with my family.
In Jesus' name.
Amen.

Ice Cream Sundae

Deuteronomy 26:1–10

Sam's eyes grew wide and a big grin spread over his face as the waitress placed his treat before him. Immediately, he dug into the hot fudge sundae with whipped cream and a maraschino cherry on top. He must have been extremely hungry. Not once did he offer to share his sundae with us.

We watched wistfully as Sam gulped down the cherry, devoured the whipped cream, and slurped up the fudge and ice cream. Finally, as he reached the bottom of his dish, Sam started to slow down. Eventually, all that remained of the delicious treat were a few spoonfuls of melted ice cream and soupy syrup.

"I'm full," Sam announced. "You can finish it."

Thanks, Son. How generous of you!

In the Old Testament, God commanded the Israelites to bring their firstfruits of crops and livestock to the tabernacle as an offering. God gave this commandment so the Israelites would remember that all their blessings, even their very lives, were gifts from their loving Creator and Provider.

God also asks us Christians to share the firstfruits of our time, income, and talents. Unfortunately, we sometimes resemble Sam eating his sundae when it comes to offering God what He deserves. Many weeks we devour our income, using it to take care of our own (or our family's) needs. If we have a few dollars left over, we drop them in the offering plate. Too often those dollars don't amount to much. We may spend countless hours working and taking care of our families, and then feel too tired to take time for prayer and Bible study. We gulp down the sundae and offer God the soupy remains.

Thankfully, God doesn't do the same for us. Whenever we call out to God, He responds to us immediately, and takes time to listen to our every word. Best of all, when God saw the mess we humans made of the world, He sent us the best, the *crème de la crème,* Jesus Christ, His Son, to save us. When we remember that God was willing to give us the ultimate firstfruit, He works through us to give back more than leftovers. We gratefully give God our best, our firstfruits, knowing that everything we have is a gift from our loving Creator—the Source of all our blessings.

God,

giver of all good things,
You spared no expense in giving us the very best—
our Savior Jesus Christ.

In response to Your loving gift,
help us in return to give our very best
in service to You and Your Church.
In Jesus' name.
Amen.

Baby Talk

Romans 8: 22–27

When our son was first learning to talk, he passed through a stage that was awkward and frustrating for all of us. He was eager to communicate his needs and desires to us. However, his grasp of language was still limited. When Sam became especially excited, he would forget the small amount of English he knew and grunt.

If Sam spotted a cookie on the counter, he would wave his finger furiously while uttering, "Uh, uh, uh!" We had to guess what he was trying to tell us.

"You hurt your finger?"

"Nuh, uh. Nuh, uh."

"You want something on the counter?"

"Uhhh! Uhhh!"

"You want one of those bananas?"

"Nuhhh!"

On it would go, until we either succeeded in understanding Sam or he gave up in frustration. Our communication problems with our son reminded us of our efforts to talk with God. Sometimes our attempts at prayer sound much like Sam's "baby talk." In fact, St. Paul describes human attempts at communicating with God as "groaning." He writes: "We know that the whole creation has been groaning as in the pains of childbirth right up to the present time" (Romans 8:22). Paul goes on to write, "the Spirit helps us in our weakness. We do not know what we ought to pray for, but the Spirit Himself intercedes for us with groans that words cannot express" (Romans 8:26).

Like Sam, we don't always know what's good for us. (He didn't really need that cookie now, did he?) We sometimes have trouble distinguishing true needs from mere desires. And in our eagerness to ask God for what we so desperately want, our prayers sometimes sound like a bunch of grunts and groans: "Uh, Lord, uh, hmm, uh, please ..."

The good news is that unlike human parents, God always knows exactly what we're asking for. God also knows exactly what we need and promises to provide for us.

Sam sometimes gave up in frustration when trying to communicate with us. We don't need to quit praying, however, just because the words don't come out right. God commands us to pray. Paul reminds us, "in everything, by prayer and petition, with thanksgiving, present your requests to God" (Philippians 4:6).

We don't need to be eloquent. Sometimes we don't even need to use words (unlike human parents, our heavenly Father can read minds and see deep into our hearts). But we do need to pray. Every day. When we come before God in the name of our Savior Jesus Christ, the Holy Spirit helps us to distinguish our true needs from mere desires. God hears our frustrated groaning and gives us the "peace of God, which transcends all understanding" (Philippians 4:7).

Heavenly Father,

You know my needs better than I do.
Provide me with words for my feelings.
Remind me each day to share all my concerns
with You.

In Jesus' name.

Amen.

Family Tree

Hebrews 11:1–12:2

A few years ago, while enjoying dinner at the home of friends, we noticed a framed poster with hundreds of names written in calligraphy. "What's that?" we inquired. Our friends told us that their 14-year-old son, Matthew, had become interested in their family history that summer. With the help of his uncle, a historian, he had traced their family's genealogy to 1400.

We asked Matthew to tell us about the names. He shared some amazing stories with us about the people in his family. Besides finding the bare facts, the names and the dates, he interviewed relatives and read old journals. Matthew had gathered an entire family history.

We all have a history to gather. If we sat down with members of our extended family and start to ask questions, we could probably begin to set down our own family tree. We could learn the stories upon which our family's traditions have been built. Then, as we come to difficult junctures in our own lives, we could ask ourselves, "What did Grandma do when this happened to her?" It helps to know that the generations before us have encountered similar trials and tribulations. It's a bonus if we can also know how they handled life's difficulties.

As Christians, we are also part of a larger family. The writer of the letter to the Hebrews called it the "great cloud of witnesses" (Hebrews 12:1), all those who have gone in faith before us. We don't need to dig through dusty libraries to discover their stories. They have already been recorded for us in one volume. The Bible tells of the adventures of our spiritual ancestors, those women and men whom God loved and guided in ages past. As we read and share their stories, we learn lessons for our own lives. Sometimes we gain courage from their faithful acts. Sometimes we learn from their mistakes. Just like us, our spiritual ancestors were far from perfect, but their flaws and failings never stopped God from caring for them.

Our Biblical family provides us with many lessons for parenting. From Sarah and Abraham we learn the heartache of infertility and the eventual joy of receiving a long-promised gift. Samuel's mother, Hannah, teaches us that our children are never really our own to control or keep. Her willingness to dedicate Samuel to work and live in the Lord's temple can give us courage when we need to allow our own children to step out into the world (1 Samuel 1:21–28). On the other hand, the experience of Eli, the priest, reminds us what can happen when our children rebel from God's ways (1 Samuel 2:12–25). From Jacob and Rebekah we learn the dangers of playing favorites with our children (Genesis 27).

In the gospels, we can draw inspiration from the faithfulness of Mary and the devotion of Jesus' step-father, Joseph. We see a Canaanite woman who cares so compassionately for her demon-possessed daughter she boldly approaches Jesus and asks for His healing power (Matthew 15:21–28). We hear Jesus' poignant reminder from the cross that in the Christian family we are not related by our own blood but by the very blood of Christ (John 19:25–27).

We are surrounded by a great cloud of witnesses—our Christian family tree. The cross is the tree that binds us together and makes us the family of God.

Thank You, gracious God,

for the gift of Your holy Word and the stories
it tells about my spiritual ancestors.
Let me learn from their examples as I pass
on the story of Your love to my own children.
In Jesus' name.
Amen.

Family Time

Ephesians 4:2–6; Hebrews 10:25

In our house, we call them "family times." They are those special moments when we temporarily put aside all our individual pursuits and spend time together as a family. We have come to treasure these moments. "Family time" may take the form of a meal, a walk to the park, and on special occasions, an outing in the car. We have discovered that we need to make family time a regular, consistent part of each day, even if it lasts only a few minutes.

Family times serve a basic yet essential function in our lives. They remind us that we love and value one another. They give us the emotional nourishment we need to take on life's daily challenges. In the midst of attending to some of our least favorite parental tasks, like washing clothes and fixing broken toys, we remember our family times and find inspiration to continue our work.

As Christians, we also need to take family time. We need to be together with our sisters and brothers in Christ for moments of worship, Bible study, and prayer. If we neglect to spend time with our broader family of faith, we may soon forget God's purpose for our daily lives.

Week after week, we gather with other believers to lift our voices in praise of Christ, feast at our Lord's Table, and listen attentively to the preaching of God's Word. As we participate in these events, we remember that we are all children of the same heavenly Father.

When children are born into this world, whatever the circumstances, they are received into some sort of family, people who provide for their needs. When we are baptized, we are born again into a second family—the body of Christ, our brothers and sisters in the Lord. During a baptism, parents and godparents promise to bring their children to worship at God's house and provide for their instruction in the Christian faith. In essence, they are promising to make sure their children spend some regular Christian "family time" with other believers.

We are thankful for our Christian family time. We are blessed by a Savior whose acts of love have transformed total strangers into our very own sisters and brothers. We are related by Christ's blood, a bond that is stronger than any other on this earth.

Thank You, Jesus,
for giving me two families to love—
my family at home
and the family I meet in my church home.
Bless the time I spend with each of them.

Amen.

Grown-Up Children

Ephesians 4:14–15; 1 Corinthians 14:20

"Once a parent, always a parent." This is a favorite saying of one of our friends. She speaks from experience. She is the mother of four sons, all of whom are now adults.

On a recent morning, we stopped at her home while her youngest son, James, was visiting. He lives 500 miles away, works for a law firm, has been married for seven years, and has two sons of his own. But you wouldn't have known it had you met him for the first time that morning.

James sat at the kitchen table in his bathrobe while his mother served him a breakfast of pancakes and bacon. She flitted back and forth, catering to her son's every need. First she brought him a napkin. Then she filled his coffee cup. When he dropped his fork on the floor, she swooped down to pick it up and brought him a new one.

"Now Jimmy, dear," she said, "I ironed your shirt. I found an old tie of your father's that matches it perfectly."

James peered up at us with an embarrassed grin on his face. "Sometimes Mom forgets that I'm all grown up," he said. Then he admitted, "I don't mind. After all, I don't receive this kind of attention at home."

Once a parent, always a parent.

In many ways, our relationship with God is similar to that of James and his mother. When our heavenly Father establishes a relationship with us through our Baptism into Christ, He promises to be our Father forever. Whether we're 2 or 92, God promises to provide for all our daily needs and to comfort us in times of trouble. Although our earthly parents may sometimes fail us, our heavenly Father will not.

God remains our Father forever, and we continue to be God's children. As Christians, we retain a childlike spirit, which enables us to trust and rely on God. Even so, as we grow in years, the Holy Spirit enables us to mature in our relationship with God through Christ. Our heavenly Father calls us to become adult children of God.

St. Paul describes this calling beautifully when he writes: "Then we will no longer be infants, tossed back and forth by the waves, and blown here and there by every wind of teaching and by the cunning and craftiness of men in their deceitful scheming. Instead, speaking the truth in love, we will in all things grow up into Him who is the Head, that is, Christ" (Ephesians 4:14–15).

As you watch your own children grow and mature, ask yourself: are you also maturing in your relationship with your heavenly Father through Jesus Christ? Are you becoming a "grown-up Christian"?

Heavenly Father,

I thank You for the relationship
You began with me on the day I was baptized.

As I continue to grow older each day,
nurture my growth in faith in You.
In Jesus' name.
Amen.

When We Turn Away

Hosea 11:1-9

It was almost suppertime. Our son, an avid book lover, sat in an aisle at one of those super-sized bookstores with six or seven books spread out in front of him. "Time to go," we called. "No!" shouted Sam. He grabbed three of the books and bolted to another part of the store. We called his name, but Sam continued to run as far away from us as he could. "I don't want to leave my books," he cried.

In the Old Testament, the people of Israel are often described as disobedient children who turned away from God. The prophet Hosea records a beautiful speech in which God laments the children's leaving. God speaks of teaching the children to walk, gathering them up in His arms, and healing them. God tells how He led the children "with cords of human kindness, with ties of love. I lifted the yoke from their neck and bent down to feed them" (Hosea 11:4).

As parents, we know what it is like to pour our effort and energy into raising our children, only to have them turn 2 or 12 or 18 and step out into independence. While this is a healthy step, and absolutely necessary for a child's development, it can be accompanied by not-so-healthy habits.

One friend's son turned 13 and announced he was done with attending church. A colleague admitted being flabbergasted when she found signs her daughter had been smoking. All parents have to deal with their children stepping out on their own, and in different ways, stepping away from their family's values.

Because God has dealt with His children's turning away, because God knows both the hopes and disappointments of being a parent, we can turn to God for guidance and encouragement. Through the Bible, we can learn that God acts with patience and love toward His temperamental children. Although we all disobey God time and again, He never abandons us. No matter how far we may try to run, God never stops pursuing us!

When we are feeling less than patient with our own children, we can ask God to remind us that this stubborn toddler or sullen teenager was once a cooing little baby whom we cuddled and fed. We can pray that God will remind us of our own wanderings and the many times He has found us. We can recall that God loved us enough to send Jesus to die for our sins that we might have new life with Him. God loves us like a perfect parent and through that love teaches us how to care for our own children.

Heavenly Father,

    when parenting becomes a challenge,
    make my words
    and actions a reflection of Yours—
        patient,
            forgiving,
                and loving.
                    In Jesus' name. Amen.

Selective Listening

2 Timothy 3:14–17

What's with kids these days? You tell them once, you tell them twice, and by the third time you can barely refrain from shouting: "Clean your room!" (or "Do your homework!" or "Take out the garbage!") You start to wonder if they have a hearing problem, because no matter how many times you speak to them, you seem to get no reaction.

The strange thing is that you can be on one side of your home and they can be on the other, and all you need to do is whisper, "I just made chocolate chip cookies," (or "Do you want to go to the mall?" or "I've got tickets to the ballgame."), and they come running.

What's with kids these days? They don't have a hearing problem, they have a *selective* hearing problem. It's not just children who suffer from this ailment. On one level or another, most of us hear only what we *want* to hear. We tune out the rest.

It's not a recent phenomenon. The Bible tells us Adam and Eve also had a selective hearing problem. God told Adam, "You are free to eat from any tree in the garden" (Genesis 2:16). Adam heard those words loud and clear. God also said, "but you must not eat from the tree of the knowledge of good and evil, for when you eat of it you will surely die" (Genesis 2:17). Adam must have tuned out that part. Well, maybe he heard it, but it sure didn't sink in (see Genesis 3:1–7).

Many of us listen to God's Word selectively. In the Bible, God speaks to us in words that are sometimes challenging, sometimes comforting, but always inspired and true. We dare not ignore any part of what God has said.

Sometimes we only hear God's challenging words. We hear God's law, words that convict us of our sin and remind us of how we disappoint God. When this happens, we stagger through life, obsessed with our guilt, unable to receive the message we need to hear more than any other—that God sent Jesus to die for our sins and restore our relationship with Him.

At other times, we have no trouble hearing this message of grace. We tune out God's law, forgetting that God has given us standards to live by. In these moments, we need to remember Paul's words to the Romans: "Shall we go on sinning so that grace may increase? By no means! We died to sin; how can we live in it any longer?" (Romans 6:1–2).

As parents, we speak both challenging and comforting words to our children. Sometimes we chastise them. Sometimes we encourage them. Always we hope to help them. Likewise, when God speaks to us as His children, God always does so with our best interests in mind.

Holy God,
gracious God,

open our ears that we may hear Your Word
    and
    respond to it with joy.
        In Jesus' name.

    Amen.

Toys Don't Last

Luke 12:13–21

We had left our son alone to entertain himself in his playroom while we were talking in the kitchen. We were deeply involved in our conversation. Suddenly, we realized a full 20 minutes had passed since we had last heard from Sam.

When you are the parents of a 3-year-old, you know that if your son has been quietly entertaining himself for more than five minutes, it's usually not good news. We were especially concerned since Sam had a newfound interest in inserting objects other than videotapes into the VCR.

When we stepped into the playroom, the first things we saw were the mountains of toys. Stuffed animals, model trucks, balls, books, puppets, wooden trains, plastic farm animals, blocks, and various other toys lay scattered on the floor. In the middle of this mess, Sam sat with his head in a book—his toddler picture Bible. He was reading over and over to himself the story of Jesus calming the sea.

We should have taken a picture. Then we could look at that picture whenever we need to remember what's most important in our lives. Since Sam was a baby, we have tried to limit the number of toys he owns. We have constantly reminded both him and ourselves that God entrusts our material possessions to us as gifts. We don't want to hoard them or value them too dearly. Sam, however, has generous grandparents and friends. He also lives in a materialistic society where all of us are bombarded with the message that we need to accumulate more and more if we want to be truly happy.

As we talk with other Christian parents, we find that like us, they struggle to teach their children to love God more than possessions. Jesus said, "Take care! Be on your guard against all kinds of greed; for one's life does not consist in the abundance of possessions" (Luke 12:15 NRSV).

As loving parents, we want to provide for our children's physical needs. We want them to live well. We enjoy watching them play with their toys (and sometimes we enjoy playing with those toys ourselves!).

Yet if we really love our children, we will take time to teach them about the One who is the source of every blessing. We will tell them all about Jesus and how He lived, died, and rose to life again to forgive their sins and establish an everlasting relationship with them.

Toys don't last. Our relationship with our Savior Jesus Christ will endure forever. Pray that both you and your children can proclaim with St. Paul: "I consider everything a loss compared to the surpassing greatness of knowing Christ Jesus my Lord" (Philippians 3:8).

Precious Savior,
teach me that You are really all I need.

Amen.

Comparisons

Luke 15:11–31

"Why can't you be more like Brian?"

"Your sister is eating it, you eat it too."

We've all heard comments like these. Maybe from our own parents, grandparents, or teachers. We've listened to other parents speak these words on the playground or at church. Many of us have said them ourselves: "Why can't I be more like ..."

As parents, we may also hear words of comparison from our children: "Why didn't I get a hug? I'm scared too!" "Why do I have to go to bed now? Julie's parents let her stay up as late as she wants."

From birth, we compare our children to other children. We gather with other parents and talk about those early achievements—teething, sleeping through the night, gaining weight. It's hard not to brag. We are tempted to rank these babies with test-like precision, predicting which ones are Ivy-League bound. But the comparisons don't end then. As they grow, we continue to compare our children to other children, aloud and in front of them. They hear what we say and then they begin to do the same thing to themselves. They may look at their siblings and wonder who Mom and Dad loves more.

In Jesus' parable of the prodigal son, the older son stays while the younger son takes his inheritance and runs off to find his happiness. When the younger returns, the father rejoices and throws a party. The older son, seething with anger, says to his father, "Look! All these years I've been slaving for you and never disobeyed your orders. Yet you never gave me even a young goat so I could celebrate with my friends. But when this son of yours who has squandered your property with prostitutes comes home, you kill the fattened calf for him!" (Luke 15:29-30).

The older son can see only the *differences* between how the father treated his brother and himself. He is asking, "Do you really love me as much as you love my brother?" The father answers, "My son ... you are always with me, and everything I have is yours" (Luke 15:31).

When we compare ourselves to others, we may only see how we do not measure up. We can easily become focused upon what we think we lack. The father in this story tries to refocus the elder son's attention to the many blessings he has. That's a healthy antidote to comparisons. When we are tempted to rail at God about what we don't have, He helps us take a step back and look at all we have. It might be time to look at our children and thank God for the gift of who they are (instead of wishing they were more like someone else). It might be time to look at ourselves and praise God for creating us just as we are (rather than wasting our time longing to look and act like our favorite movie star).

God has blessed each of us with the gift of life. God has created us as unique individuals with specific purposes in His kingdom on this earth. One way we can show our love to God is by daily offering our gratitude. When we ponder all of our blessings, we begin to see how richly God has provided for us and forget to worry about what we think we lack.

Thanks be to God!

Prayer idea:
Make a list of some of the ways
God has blessed you.

Then pray,
naming each item on your list and saying,

"Thank You, gracious God."

Ask, Seek, Knock

Matthew 7:7–11

We can learn a lot about persistence from our children. Our son has found that a combination of sheer repetition and increased volume works for him. When Sam wants to do something, like go outside and ride in his toy car, he will make up a little song about it. "Ride in the C-A-R. Ride, ride in the C-A-R. Mommy. Mommy. Mommy. Let's ride in the C-A-R!" Sam sings the song over and over, louder each time, until we at least acknowledge his request.

Jesus encouraged persistence. In His sermon on the mount, Jesus gives this directive: "Ask and it will be given to you; seek and you will find; knock and the door will be opened to you. For everyone who asks receives; he who seeks finds; and to him who knocks, the door will be opened" (Matthew 7:7–8). Jesus then gives the example of parents and their children. He tells His listeners that if they, who are sinful, are able to give good gifts to their children, then most certainly our gracious heavenly Father will give good gifts to those who ask Him.

Jesus' words make it sound easy. And it is. We are invited to bring everything to God. Unfortunately, we often do every-thing *but* talk to God about our concerns. We complain to our spouses. We discuss our problems with our friends and co-workers. We read self-help books. We call radio talk shows looking for answers. None of these tactics is wrong in and of themselves. Our problem is we often forget to try the one thing that really can help the most—prayer.

Jesus' words suggest more than just a prayer mumbled at bedtime, though certainly that will help. Jesus encourages con-tinual and persistent calling on God with our problems. Jesus tells us to present our concerns to God morning, noon, and night. We may not get the answer we desire, but God will certainly hear our prayers and give us the answer we need. As we share our concerns with God, He helps us distinguish between what we really need and what we *think* we need.

Many of us use the excuse, "I'm too busy to pray." Most of us are too busy *not* to pray. With the hectic pace and constant demands of family life, we need the peace only Jesus provides. We need to worship in divine service, praying with the community of believers and receiving communion at the Lord's Table. We need to take time in those minutes just after we wake and just before we fall asleep to whisper our thanks and make our requests known to God. And in those small, quiet moments, in the car or while washing dishes, those in-between moments when doubts or worries start to plague us, we can mumble our requests to God. Ask, seek, and knock. God will most certainly provide.

Thank You, Father,
for promising to listen
to me always
and to provide me
with exactly what I need.
In Jesus' name.
Amen.

It Takes a Village

Philemon

An old saying goes: "It takes a village to raise a child." St. Paul wrote, "Carry each other's burdens" (Galatians 6:2). He also compared the Christian Church to a body in which all the parts work together to honor Christ (1 Corinthians 12). Passages like these remind us that we are never alone in our parenting tasks. Ideally, we have extended family members to help us. Beyond that, we need other people: our neighbors and friends, our church community, and those who live in our village, town, or city. All of us—pastors and teachers, store clerks and firefighters, parents and grandparents—work together to raise up our children.

In Philemon, a little book nestled between Titus and Hebrews, St. Paul wrote to Philemon, Apphia, Archippus, and their church on behalf of Onesimus, a runaway slave: "I appeal to you for my son Onesimus, who became my son while I was in chains" (Philemon 10). Paul pleaded Onesimus' case, hopeful that Philemon would welcome him back as a brother instead of a slave. Clearly, Paul had mentored this young man. They had developed a relationship close enough for Paul to refer to Onesimus as his son even though they were not related by blood.

Since we have become parents, many others have offered care and love to our son: our parents and siblings, his Sunday school teachers, his Sunday school classmates, youth group members, and our friends. Through the years, we have also, in small ways, taken on the responsibility of caring for the children of others. When children at our church have seemed sad or worried, we have offered our time to listen to them. When our friends have had second children, we have provided a quiet afternoon "getaway" at our house for the older sibling, a place to feel special and honored in the midst of all the newness at home. These are small acts. Yet they are ways we seek to fulfill God's commandment to love our neighbor and carry one another's burdens. They remind us that as Christians we are not sailing the seas of life alone. We sail together, in a fleet of vessels, guided and protected by our Savior.

When we say, "it takes a village," we must remember that the most important part of that village is God. We cannot count the many times we have grumbled about how difficult parenting is, how alone we feel. As we toss sullied sheets in the wash at three in the morning, a feverish child in our arms, we may feel like we are carrying our burdens by ourselves. But even then, midway through the night, God is there to strengthen us. We are never alone. God has given us the community of faith. We have a village, the body of Christ, our sisters and brothers in the Lord. We carry each other's burdens. As we do so, God lifts us up and gives us strength to go on.

Gracious and loving God,
when I feel alone,
sustain me with Your presence.

Send me into the community of faith
where I can receive the care of my neighbors,
and in turn, love others.
In Jesus' name.
Amen.

"You Are What You Eat"

Philippians 4:8–9

Rochelle's grandmother said it all the time. "You are what you eat." She also said, "Garbage in, garbage out."

She was talking mostly about junk food. She also wasn't fond of television. She said it would rot our brains. She had similar sentiments about those movie magazines for teenagers. Now that we are parents of a little one, we see her point. Truthfully, her sentiment applies to more than just food.

Many athletes say eating the right food can help produce outstanding physical results (and eating the wrong food before a race or a game can be a disaster). But it goes deeper than that. As writers, we have learned that if we hope to produce powerful and well-crafted words, we need to read the best literature available. We can't feast all night on prime-time television and expect to rise in the morning and write great prose.

As children and as parents, what we hear about ourselves from the media, our families, and our friends often becomes a message we repeat to ourselves throughout the day. If we watch a lot of television, we might receive the message that we need to buy more clothes and use the right products to become beautiful. If we hear criticism all day, no matter who says it, we can easily begin to believe it and think less of ourselves. If we fill our hearts and minds with messages of hate, violence, and despair we may begin to feel hopeless.

In his letter to the Philippians, Paul reminds us: "whatever is true, whatever is noble, whatever is right, whatever is pure, whatever is lovely, whatever is admirable—if anything is excellent or praiseworthy—think about such things" (Philippians 4:8). As parents, the Holy Spirit uses us to help our children put Paul's words into practice in their daily lives. We can monitor their television viewing and computer use. We can play Christian music at home and in the car. We can provide a daily quiet time for family Bible reading and discussion. As we talk with our children, we can encourage them and show genuine interest in their lives.

A colleague of ours struggled through a difficult time in his relationship with his son. He vowed to himself that out of love, he would start to listen to his son without constantly correcting or criticizing him. It proved to be a brilliant solution. His son felt encouraged and loved and began to relate to his father in a whole new way.

Of course, everything in this world that is true, noble, and pure originates with God. We cannot expect our children to develop healthy attitudes and habits if they do not receive regular doses of God's Word. If you make a habit of dining on junk food, eating one healthy meal a week will not result in a balanced diet. Likewise, if your children aren't exposed to God's Word during their daily lives at home, an hour of church or Sunday school will hardly sustain them.

What kind of messages are your children receiving each day? Are they gulping down garbage or being nourished by God's good news?

Dear Jesus,
> whatever is true,
> whatever is pure,
> whatever is lovely ...
> let me think about such things.
> Amen.

Opportunities!

Matthew 25:14–30

Two women were talking. The first woman said, "I think God can do great things with pain and suffering. I know that I grow more when I am in pain than when my life is going smoothly. Maybe we need to think of our pain as an opportunity." The second woman replied, "Good point, but let me tell you something ... I am getting sick of having all these opportunities!"

As parents, life presents us with many "opportunities" for growth. Each day brings new trials. We have found that as soon as we hit a comfortable stride, an "opportunity" appears and we stumble. Our child gets sick, the car breaks down, the computer crashes, or someone spills red punch on the new white rug. It doesn't take much to trip us. The results often depend upon how we respond to these "opportunities."

In the parable of the talents, Jesus tells the story of a man going on a journey. Before he departs, he leaves talents—or money—to three of his servants. The first servant "put his money to work" (Matthew 25:16) and doubled it. The second servant did the same. The third servant, out of fear, "dug a hole in the ground and hid his master's money" (Matthew 25:18). When the master returns, he commends the first two servants and condemns the third.

In this parable, the talents represent all God has given us: our time, our abilities, and our possessions. God calls us to take all of this and put it to good use so it multiplies for the good of His kingdom. This means that those of us who can sing, teach, or bake can do so in ways that glorify God. The same goes for those of us who can sew, fix toys, write stories, or care for children. We implore the Holy Spirit to direct us, to guide us in using our talents in the best possible way. Then, as

God works through us to share our talents, we experience His blessings. Everything we do, we do to glorify God.

This brings us full circle to the question of life's challenges or "opportunities." The third servant hid his talent because he was afraid. " 'Master,' he said, 'I knew that you are a hard man, harvesting where you have not sown and gathering where you have not scattered seed. So I was afraid and went out and hid your talent in the ground. See, here is what belongs to you' " (Matthew 25:24–25).

We will all encounter suffering and pain ("opportunities") in our lives. As the Bible reminds us, rain falls on everyone—the just and the unjust (Matthew 5:45). Yet we worship a God who is able to turn life's darkest moments into glorious opportunities. If God can transform this world's most horrific event—Jesus' death—into the ultimate plan of salvation, then no doubt God can also bring new opportunities out of our daily disappointments.

Our task as Christians is to ask God to help us respond to these situations in the best possible way. As the Holy Spirit leads us, we can begin to see each difficulty as an opportunity for our faith to grow. In those times, God will give us the courage to keep going. God will steady and strengthen us. Like a parent holding the back of our bicycle, God will not let go until we are again ready to ride on our own.

Gracious God,

thank You for all You have given me.
Encourage me to use my gifts to glorify You.
Assure me that the problems I face are merely
opportunities to grow in love
and obedience to You.
In Jesus' name.
Amen.

Rewind, Part 1

Psalm 143:5–6

In an effort to limit our son's television viewing time and control its content, we purchased a number of videotapes for him to watch. These tapes include some of his favorite story characters as well as full-length children's movies. Sam is allowed to watch only a certain number of these tapes each week. Sam is a clever child, however. He has learned that one way he can stretch out his video viewing time is by asking us to rewind the tape so he can view his favorite scenes a second time.

When Sam first asked us to rewind a scene, we thought nothing of it. It was a scene in a movie Sam found absolutely hilarious. We had no idea what Sam was laughing at. (Three-year-old humor goes over our heads). But Sam has an infectious giggle and soon we were laughing with him. So when he asked us to rewind to the scene again, we eagerly obliged.

We ended up returning to the scene four or five times. All the while Sam rolled on the floor and giggled. Thus was the phrase, "Rewind it, please," born in our house. We've since put a limit on the number of times a scene from one of Sam's videos can be replayed (no matter how funny it may be).

All humans enjoy replaying favorite moments from their lives over and over again. That's what memories are all about. That's why we collect our favorite photos and put them into albums. That's why we tell stories. (Just count all the times the word "remember " appears in the Bible!)

When we gather for worship week after week and listen to familiar stories about Jesus, it's like hitting the rewind button. Every year we relive the events of our Savior's life.

During the dark days of December, we go back in time more than 2000 years to recall that moment when Jesus entered this world. Born in a manger of a virgin mother. Visited by Magi and shepherds. Every year, we play that story over and over, and yet it never loses its power.

Every spring during Holy Week, we revisit the last days of our Lord's life on this earth. The parade of palms held in His honor as He entered Jerusalem. The last supper with His disciples, a moment we remember every time we gather for Holy Communion. Our Lord's anguish in Gethsemane. Judas' betrayal with a kiss. Jesus' arrest and trial. The long, agonizing walk to Golgotha. Those dreadful hours on the cross. The terrible silence of death. Then the moment that changed history forever—our Lord alive again! Alive forever!

It doesn't matter how many times we replay them, those stories still send chills down our spines. As we share them with our children, our neighbors, and the whole world, we are reminded of how much our God loves us. We are reminded of all He's done to save us. See, rewind isn't such a bad idea!

Lord Jesus,
thank You for the gift of memory.
Rewind me,
and
remind me daily
of all You have done for me
through Your life,
death,
and resurrection.
Amen.

Rewind, Part 2

Luke 2:1–20

Although we mostly use our television for viewing videos, we do allow our son to tune into a few of his favorite shows. One day he was watching *Sesame Street* and his favorite song came on. When the song was over, Sam turned to us and said, "Rewind it, please. I want to see it again."

We tried to explain that we couldn't rewind something if it wasn't on tape. Sam didn't understand. We're expecting that some day he'll ask us to rewind real-life events. "Can you rewind Christmas?" "My birthday party?" "Our trip to Grandma and Grandpa's house?"

Can you imagine what life would be like if we actually *could* rewind our days? Which moments would you choose to live a second or even a third time? We all experience those once-in-a-lifetime moments that are so delicious we'd like to replay them again and again. Some of them are the big events—graduations, weddings, and births. Many of them come as quiet surprises—the first time our child says, "I love you;" an unexpected gift from our spouse; a visit from a long lost friend. All of them say something about our lives, a truth we want to treasure for the rest of our days on this earth.

Imagine that we could rewind our lives and experience some of those special events again. Do you think we'd all get stuck on reliving certain moments and never move on?

In the Christmas story, St. Luke tells how Mary responded to the events of our Savior's birth: "But Mary treasured up all these things and pondered them in her heart" (Luke 2:19). Much like any mother after giving birth and welcoming visitors, she retreated at the end of the day to "treasure" and "ponder" all that had happened.

We wonder if Mary revisited this moment throughout her

life. As Jesus was dying on the cross, harassed by a hostile crowd, was Mary remembering a very different crowd, the ones who bowed before Him on the night of His birth? We don't know. However, we do know that Mary remained a part of Jesus' life throughout His ministry. Unlike most of His disciples, she did not flee when He was crucified. Whether she wanted to rewind or not, Mary stuck with the One who was both her son and her Savior, even in His most painful moments.

Mary's life can be a lesson for us all. Some days we encounter are so precious, so wonderful, that we may be tempted to romanticize them, to try to hold on to them forever, and say: this is what I wish each day could be like. In truth, all our days are precious and jam-packed with God's blessings. At the end of each day, we can follow Mary's example as we "treasure up" and "ponder" the day's events. We open our hearts to God in our nightly prayers and speak a heartfelt "thank You" for all our blessings. Then we can ask our risen Savior to help us move on, knowing He is always present in the present, and through every moment of our lives.

Creator God,

thank You for the gift of this moment.
Show me its beauty so I do not long for the past.
In Jesus' name.

Amen.

Fast Forward

Romans 5:1–5

Now that we've spoken the praises of the modest technological advancement known as the rewind button, we'd like to consider another feature of our VCR—fast forward. Our son discovered fast forward when he encountered a frightening scene in his favorite movie. First, he tried covering his eyes with his hands and shouting, "No!" When that didn't work, he ran to his mother and said, "Don't like it. Make it go away." Soon, Sam learned that with a touch of a button, he could make both the frightening and the boring parts of his videos go speeding by until he found a scene he liked.

No doubt, we have all encountered moments when we have wished we could control our own lives with a fast forward button. How wonderful we think it would be to simply skip over life's unpleasant moments. If we hate our jobs, then we could speed through the work week and jump from weekend to weekend. We would fast forward through those moments when the children are screaming and stop at those pleasant times when they're so adorable we want to hug them and never let go. Sound like a great idea? Well, according to God, it's not.

Though we all experience moments we would rather avoid, every single second in our lives is important. The Bible reminds us that because we belong to Christ, even those moments when we suffer or encounter difficulties can be times of growth and blessing (see Romans 5:3–5). Because we belong to Christ, God promises to watch over us and guide wherever we go and whatever we do (see Psalm 139:1–10). Every moment of our life is important to God, whether we're cleaning the oven or vacationing in the Bahamas.

One of our tasks as parents involves helping our children to encounter life's less pleasant moments. We teach them that when they play with toys, they also need to put them away. If they want to receive an allowance, they need to help with household chores. As we teach our children these life lessons, we can help them see that God blesses every moment of their lives, even those moments they would rather avoid.

While fast forward may be a wonderful feature on VCRs, we don't think it would be helpful in real life. Imagine what our world would be like if God had simply fast forwarded through the hours of our Savior's death. Those dark hours on Calvary were the most horrible moments this world has ever experienced. Yet without them, there would be no resurrection, no salvation for this world, no hope for its future. And because Christ suffered, because He encountered death and the devil and emerged victorious, we live in His victory as He helps us in our moments of weakness (see Hebrews 2:18). Christ is with us. We don't need to hit the fast forward button when times get tough.

Jesus,

> when my life feels overwhelming
> and I'm ready to hit "fast forward,"
> remind me that You are present
> in the midst of my pain.

You suffered on the cross
> and You have reconciled me to God.
> You have promised to comfort me
> in my own moments of darkness.

Thank You, Jesus, for this promise.
Amen.

Don't Forget!

Luke 12:6–7

It happens every time our family takes a trip. We pack our luggage and read through our list to make sure we haven't forgotten anything. We load the car. Then we walk through the house, checking to see that we have turned out all the lights and locked all the doors. Finally, we're off, happy travelers, ready for a relaxing vacation.

Happy—until we're a few miles down the road. Suddenly, Rochelle asks, "Did you remember to turn off the oven?"

"I forget," replies Harold.

"You mean you forgot to turn off the oven?"

"I don't remember."

Inevitably, we turn around and head back home, just to make sure.

Of course, we aren't the only ones plagued by the terrible condition of forgetfulness. All people, young and old, forget sometimes. In fact, in this modern world of ours, where most of us watch television, use computers, and read the newspaper, there are quite a number of things for us to forget. We recently heard that those of us living in the 21st century are exposed to more information in 30 days than people living 100 years ago received in their entire lifetimes. There is a lot of information floating around in our world. Frankly, much of it is not worth remembering!

Humans have always been forgetful. That's why a few thousand years ago God commanded the people of Israel to "be careful that you do not forget the LORD, who brought you out of Egypt, out of the land of slavery" (Deuteronomy 6:12). The Israelites did forget God—many times.

The same God who rescued the Israelites from slavery in

Egypt has also freed us from our bondage to sin through the death and resurrection of Jesus our Savior. Yet we, like the Israelites, are often forgetful of all that God has done for us. We forget to thank God for all the ways He provides for our families. We forget the promises we make to be God's faithful servants. We forget to confess our sins and ask God for forgiveness when we fall short of God's calling.

Despite our forgetfulness, we humans are grateful that God is not like us. God never forgets His promises. Although the Israelites failed God time and again, God never failed them. We know God will also be faithful to the promises He has made to us through our Baptism into Christ. In our sinfulness, we may forget God, but God will never forget us.

Whatever else you may forget today, be sure to remember this—you and your family are baptized. You belong to Christ. God will never forsake you.

Gracious God,

> it is wonderful to know I can trust You
> to remember all Your promises to me
> and my family, even if I forget them.

Thank You, God, for having a perfect memory!
> In Jesus' name.
> Amen.

In the World

Romans 12:1–2

We were visiting the home of friends. Their daughter, a sophomore at a Christian college, was telling us about some of her adventures at school. "College is interesting," she said. "But I know it's not the same as living in the real world."

"What do you mean by 'the real world'?" we asked.

"Like you two," she replied. "Working and raising a family and stuff. That's the real world."

Many Christians talk about how we need to "be in the world but not of the world." The phrase comes from Jesus' words about His disciples' relationship to the world in John 15 through 17 (see especially John 15:18–25). Much of the New Testament is devoted to the question of how Christians ought to live in relation to secular influences. Should we be visibly active as lights in this world, pointing people to Jesus (Matthew 5:14)? Should we be recluses, separating ourselves from "worldly ways"? Or does God want us to do some of each, to be active in the world while protecting ourselves and our children from certain influences?

Before we had a child, this issue didn't seem so pressing. We felt capable of making healthy choices for ourselves. When we became parents, we realized we needed to think about these issues in more detail. Which television shows would we allow our son to watch? What would we say about the language and jokes school children bring home from the playground? How would we teach our son about an issue dear to our hearts: living as responsible stewards in a land gone crazy with materialism? How would we teach him about serving others? Truthfully, we had more questions than answers.

Two verses serve as beacons for us as we sort through these questions on a daily basis. The first is a verse we have heard at many baptisms, as the pastor presents a candle to the child's parents: "In the same way, let your light shine before others, so that they may see your good works and give glory to your Father in heaven" (Matthew 5:16 NRSV). This verse reminds us of our purpose in the world: to be lights, living in such a way that what we do reflects Christ's love for us and all humanity. Jesus wants our words and our deeds to point beyond ourselves to God, the Source of all that is good and pleasing.

The second verse we keep before us is from Paul's letter to the church at Rome: "Do not be conformed to this world, but be transformed by the renewing of your minds, so that you may discern what is the will of God—what is good and acceptable and perfect" (Romans 12:2 NRSV). The first verse gives us our vision, a sense of what we are called to be in this world. This verse gives us the "how." Paul's words remind us that the only way we can achieve this goal is when God works to transform us.

The Holy Spirit renews our minds when we join other Christians in divine worship, receive our Savior's body and blood at the Lord's Table, and listen as God speaks to us through Scripture. As the Holy Spirit calls us to faith and guards our "hearts and minds in Christ Jesus" (Philippians 4:7), we turn away from the influences of this world. We are better able to discern God's will and are able to see what is "good and acceptable and perfect." We are able to be in the world but not of it.

Gracious God,

> guide me as I journey through this world.
> Let Your light shine through me
> so my words and actions may reflect Your love
> and illuminate the lives of others.
> In Jesus' name.
> Amen.

Seasons of Life

Ecclesiastes 3:1–8

Our son was going through one of those stages. When we made suggestions about Sam's activities, he shouted "NO!" When we reprimanded him, he threw his book. When he was hungry for cookies and *we* said "No," he would drag a chair to the cupboard and search until he found the "hidden" box of cookies.

A friend who is an expert in child development told us this was a normal stage in Sam's maturation, his "growing up." Sam needed to individuate, to separate from his parents and begin to think for himself. We very much agree with the idea of it all, but sometimes the process stinks.

The writer of Ecclesiastes reminds parents, "There is a time for everything and a season for every activity under heaven" (Ecclesiastes 3:1). In the verses that follow, the writer details these seasons of life. Reading it brings to mind an average week with a pre-schooler (or an 8-year-old or a teenager)—mourning one minute and dancing the next. It helps to normalize parenting as a life-season particularly fraught with change and growth. It reminds us that the ups and downs we experience with our children are as normal as the changing seasons of nature, as predictable as the turning of the leaves each autumn.

What seems most difficult about parenting, however, is its *unpredictability.* Sure, we know life will be different every day. We can predict *that.* We want to know *how* it will be different. Many of us would prefer these seasons of life occur on a perfect schedule. Life does not work that way. In fact, sometimes it seems family living is no more than loosely organized chaos.

In the chaos, we can hold onto something rock-solid and unchanging—God. As we move through the seasons of our lives (and our children's lives and even our parents' lives), God stands solidly beside us. On the days we want to pull out our hair or run screaming down the street, we can depend on God to give us stability and hope.

When we wake each morning, spending quiet time with God grounds us. It sets us in the right framework for a day at work or with our children. Throughout the day, brief moments of prayer (perhaps muttered between diaper changes or toy pick-up times) or a few minutes spent listening to inspirational music can calm us and renew our spirits. As we lie down to sleep each night, a prayer of gratitude to God can bring closure to the day and prepare us for the next. Truly, throughout all of life's challenge, God is the *only* One who can bring us peace and hope. God is our salvation, and in the midst of life's troubles, God is our Rock, the One who constantly supports us.

O God, You are my rock and my salvation.
Through all the seasons of my children's lives
(and through all the seasons of my own life),
support and strengthen me.
In Jesus' name.
Amen.

Where Is Jesus?

Matthew 18:20; 28:16–20

One Sunday morning, as we climbed up the stairs of the church where we worship our son asked, "Will Jesus be here today? Will Jacki be here?" Jacki is one of Sam's Sunday school friends.

"Yes, Sam," answered Rochelle, "Jesus will be here. And so will Jacki." Satisfied, Sam skipped into church and down the stairs to class.

We later talked about Sam's inquiry, discussing what we wanted to teach Sam about Jesus' presence. In Matthew's gospel, Jesus said, "For where two or three come together in My name, there I am with them" (Matthew 18:20). We want Sam to know this and more. If we were to answer Sam's question more thoroughly, we might say something like this:

"Yes, Sam, Jesus is here at church today and at many other gatherings like this around the world. Jesus is present in Baptism and God's Holy Supper. Jesus speaks through the words of the Scriptures and the sermon. Jesus sings through the voices of the choir and the congregation and flows through the melodies of the organ or guitars as the people offer praise to God.

"Jesus works through the caring patience of your mom and dad and other parents as they teach you to sing and pray. Jesus ministers through the baskets of clothes and toys you and your friends have brought to help others in need. Jesus nourishes the hungry and shelters the homeless through the hands and hearts of those who volunteer at your church.

"Yes, Sam, Jesus is here. Jesus is here for all who believe, comforting those who mourn, giving strength to the weary, filling the hearts of the faithful with joy and good cheer. Jesus was here long before you came to be, little Sam, and Jesus will be here long after you leave this earth, bringing comfort and peace to generations to come."

When our nephew was 2, his parents would ask him, "Where is Jesus?" and he would point to his heart. That is a fitting benediction to this instruction. For we also want Sam to know that Jesus is with him now, in this moment, and will continue to be with him wherever he goes.

Jesus,

> alert me to Your presence at church
> and at home,
> in my heart
> and in my hands,
> as I pray
> and as I serve.
> Amen.

The Timing Belt

Psalm 127

For the first three and a half years of our marriage, we lived in a rural area in the mountains of western Pennsylvania. We relied on our car to take us everywhere and in all kinds of weather. We logged a lot of miles, and the car experienced its share of wear and tear as it traveled up and down the mountain roads.

One frigid winter morning, Harold set off in our trusty old car to accomplish some errands. Suddenly, as he drove down the highway, everything on the car shut down—the power steering, the accelerator, even the radio. Harold managed to guide the car off the highway and ease it to the side of the road. He then bundled up and walked a mile and a half to the nearest town. Later, he learned the timing belt had broken. We're not mechanics, but we do know that when the timing belt goes, the car doesn't.

What part of our life is so important that without it we would shut down? Certainly, on a physical level, we couldn't survive without food and water. Without daily nourishment, we will eventually die. But we are much more than our physical selves; we are also spiritual beings. Without God in our lives, we would shut down completely.

Psalm 127 begins with this verse: "Unless the LORD builds the house, its builders labor in vain. Unless the LORD watches over the city, the watchmen stand guard in vain." We understand this to mean that God must be beneath and behind all we are, all we do, and all we own. Without God in our lives, we sit stalled like a car with a broken timing belt.

As parents, we sometimes feel stalled anyway. Our days are pulled by the rigorous demands of the adult world: work, bills, housework, yard work, and car care. On top of all that, we have our children to nurture and love. Some days, we walk around in a daze, wondering how much longer we can go on without sleep and nourishment, without time to care for ourselves. In this busy world, often the first thing we give up is the most necessary: our time with God. Even knowing that God is as essential to our lives as timing belts are to cars, we sometimes forget. We lose focus. We stall out.

What we need in those moments is a gentle push, maybe even a tow truck to pull us where we need to be. We need the Holy Spirit to nudge our souls. When we go to church, the Scripture lessons, the sermon, the prayers, and the hymns provide the "charge" to jump-start us. As we hear God's words of love and forgiveness and gather at our Savior's Table, we are energized to start again. We then can continue our journey on earth with God as the focal point of our lives.

Lord God, builder of my life,
focus my days
and
nights on You.
In Jesus' name I pray.
Amen.

Generosity

Mark 4:1–9

"Everybody can eat. Take as much as you want," said Mrs. Lloyd. We were celebrating the end of the Sunday school year with ice-cream sundaes. She had provided an amazing amount of toppings—candies to sprinkle and syrups to pour (as well as whipped cream to squirt). Although the church basement was packed with children, none of them went away hungry.

Many of us grew up feeling there wasn't enough to go around. We had to split desserts, share toys, and wear hand-me-down clothes. As parents, we try to provide for all of our children's needs. Sometimes, however, our resources are limited. Money, time, and patience may seem to be in short supply.

Jesus' parable of the sower portrays a remarkable side of God: His generosity. God's love is never in short supply. In Jesus' story, a sower scatters seeds that fall on four types of ground: the path, rocky ground, among thorns, and on rich soil. Seeds are expensive and not to be wasted. We can hardly imagine that a farmer would carelessly toss precious seeds about, not taking the trouble to see where they land.

Of course, this is a parable—a story that tells us something about God and our relationship to Him. It's not about a farmer who has to worry about a crop. It's about our God who wants to give us every possible chance to encounter His Word. God doesn't just cast this Word to those who are ready to hear it. God generously casts it toward everyone.

We once heard a speaker say that as we drive, we encounter mostly green lights. We don't realize this because we only notice the red ones. How true. We sometimes are astounded at how little of God's generosity we notice. Are we too busy to see God's blessings? Do we focus on the wrong things? According to the parable of the sower, God is tossing the Word with wild abandon. Are we seeing only the weeds? Are our eyes focused on the rocky ground? Are we overlooking the seeds God has planted all around us?

The parable of the sower reminds us that no matter what we experience emotionally or physically, God has sown the seeds. Even those of us who attend worship each week and pray daily sometimes wander onto rocky ground. Even when life seems unstable, God forgives us and grants us grace to go on.

Divine Sower,

I thank You for sowing Your love
through the Sacraments and Word.
Make me aware of the seeds
You have so generously sown in my life
and in the life of my family.
In Jesus' name I pray.

Amen.

I Want It NOW!

Psalm 40

"I want what I want, and I want it NOW!" we sang. This short ditty seemed to describe perfectly the attitude of our newborn son. Whether he wanted food, a diaper change, or a simple cuddle, the cry was the same: loud and urgent. As he grew, he learned a bit about delayed gratification. When he turned 3, all that went out the window. We quickly slipped back to the song of his early months: "I want what I want, and I want it NOW!"

When we shopped for groceries, Sam grabbed a box of his favorite cookies and demanded loudly, "Open it NOW!" At home, Sam frantically searched for his favorite book and shouted, "I need it NOW!" In the middle of the night, Sam woke from a deep sleep and cried, "I want to color flowers NOW!"

Sam isn't the only one in this world to demand, "I want it NOW!" Many of us adults feel and act the same way. We speed through lights turning from yellow to red, muttering, "Gotta get there, NOW!" We shop websites on the Internet, charging our purchases, exclaiming, "I gotta have it, NOW!" When we are hungry, we whip together packaged meals or hurry to the nearest drive-through. In this world of fast food and credit cards, delayed gratification seems to be a virtue of the past. We no longer *have* to wait for many things ... so why should we? What is the value in *waiting?*

As parents who pray, we have often felt the tension of being pulled between living in a fast-paced society and "waiting on the Lord." Like our son, we want our lives to answer to our demands. Of course, we hope for green lights and enjoy quick dinners, but we also find ourselves wanting God to respond at the speed of light. When we are worried about Sam or concerned about our own lives, we look to God for quick answers.

Even so, we know that our God isn't one to be rushed.

From the Bible, we know God has a history of making people wait. The Israelites were released from slavery only to wander in the wilderness for 40 years, waiting for even a glimpse of the Promised Land. During their time in exile, the people of Israel waited (again) to return to their homeland. And all that time (and longer), the Israelites waited for the Messiah to come. Even Jesus, after His birth, waited 30 years before He began His ministry. Again and again in the Scriptures, we see God's people waiting.

David reminds us that God draws us closer to Him as we wait for his answers: "I waited patiently for the LORD; He turned to me and heard my cry. ... He put a new song in my mouth, a hymn of praise to our God. Many will see and fear and put their trust in the LORD" (Psalm 40:1, 3).

Patience. It might be the hardest thing to come by at 3:00 A.M. when your child is sick, and you are praying to God for emergency help. It's even hard to be patient with God when our prayers are not emergencies. It helps to know God's Word. In the Bible, we see that although God's timing is different than our own, God always answers our prayers. In fact, God's answers, God's plans for our lives, are more amazing than we could ever imagine.

In the meantime, we pray and we wait. All the while, we remember the words of David: "Many, O LORD my God, are the wonders you have done. The things you planned for us no one can recount for you; were I to speak and tell of them they would be too many to declare" (Isaiah 40:5).

God of my ancestors,
> I sometimes want quick and easy responses
> to my prayers. Encourage me to trust patiently
> that Your answers will be worth the wait.
> In Jesus' name. Amen.

The Ladder

Romans 7:21–8:2

Our son, age 2, stood on the playground peering up at the ladder which rose like an ominous shadow before him. From Sam's vantage point, it must have looked like the top of the ladder touched the sky. Sam was not at all fond of ladders or heights. Still, he placed a foot on the first rung. "I go up," he declared.

Sam was determined that he would climb this ladder for one reason. If he made it to the top, he would reach a delightful curving slide that wound around in a spiral. What a thrill it would be to sail down this slide with his arms raised high and a gleeful shout of "Wheeee!"

Why did the only way to the top of that slide involve climbing the dreaded ladder? Sam clung to the railing. Carefully he moved his left foot up to the second rung. His body started to tremble. He let out a pitiful whine.

Still, Sam was determined to make it. Up he went, another step, higher than he had ever climbed before. Three more rungs remained between Sam and the top of the slide. There might as well have been 50. For when he glanced down at the ground and realized how far he had come, Sam froze, suddenly unable to move in any direction. Terror overwhelmed him. Tears rolled down his cheeks.

Then, from the top of the ladder a long, strong arm reached down. Before he realized what had happened, Sam had been swept up into the loving embrace of his father. Now Sam stood at the top of the ladder. His father squeezed him tightly and shouted, "Sam, you made it." Down the slide they went together, Sam's arms raised high, as father and son joined in a gleeful duet—"Whee!"

"He reached down from on high and took hold of me,"

wrote the psalmist (Psalm 18:16). The writer wasn't describing the actions of Sam's father but the saving acts of God. We humans may attempt to climb the ladder which leads to our salvation. Like Sam, however, none of us can make it to the top. Our sin paralyzes us and prevents us from moving up the ladder. On our own, we cannot reach the heights of heaven. We cannot ascend into the presence of God.

Then the long, strong arm of our Savior reaches down. Jesus, the One who was Himself lifted up on a cross (John 3:14), lifts us up. He does what we cannot.

In most religions, humans strive to become more like God to attain their salvation. As Christians, we know such an accomplishment is not possible. For that reason, God is one with us in the person of Jesus. God came down that we might be lifted up. We rest secure in our Savior's arms. Now we let out a gleeful shout—"Weee give You thanks, O God!"

Thank You, God,
for reaching down to save me
when I could not reach up.
In Jesus' blessed name,

I praise You. Amen.

Laws of Love

We were talking with the youth group at our church about a favorite teen topic—curfews.

"My parents are so strict I can't stand it," complained one boy. "They expect me to be in by 10 on weekends."

"I can't sneeze without my folks wondering what I'm up to," said another boy.

One after another, members of the youth group voiced complaints about the rules their parents imposed on them. Through it all, one girl sat silently by herself, looking a bit forlorn. After listening to 20 minutes of the gripe session, she finally spoke.

"I think curfews are a good idea," she said.

"What do you mean?" someone asked.

"I wish I had a curfew," she continued. "My mom doesn't care where I am on Friday night. Of course, she's drunk most of the time. At least your parents care enough to worry about you."

Suddenly everyone else fell silent.

Many teenagers are not fond of family rules. They often feel restricted by them. But as parents, we make rules to protect our children. We tell them not to play in the street or touch the oven because we love them. We do not want them to get hurt.

God also makes rules for His children because God loves us. Some people think God gave us the Ten Commandments to make our lives difficult. In fact, it is quite the opposite. If we all kept God's laws, our lives would be much more pleasant and our world would be a better place to live. It's when we break the commandments that we bring difficulties upon ourselves and others.

The psalmist proclaimed, "Oh, how I love your law!" (Psalm 119:97) Throughout the Old Testament, the people of Israel recognized that God's law was a gift to them. Though they did not always follow God's commands, they acknowledged that ultimately God knew what was best for them.

God also knows what's good for us. God gives us laws to make our lives better. Of course, none of us can keep God's laws perfectly. In this way, God's rules serve another, even more important, purpose. They show us our guilt and send us to our knees. They remind us that we can do nothing to save ourselves. They send us to the very foot of the cross, where we fall on the mercy of God and turn to our only hope of salvation, our Savior Jesus Christ.

Like any caring parent, God gives us rules because He loves us. God's laws are good. And God's grace is even better. "This is how we know what love is: Jesus Christ laid down His life for us" (1 John 3:16).

I thank You, Lord God,

> for caring about me so much
> that You give me Your law to guide me.
> And when I break that law,
> I thank You all the more
> for sending Your Son
> to save me.

In His name I pray.
Amen.

Teaching the Commandments

Matthew 5:17–20

When we were children, we both thought many of the Ten Commandments did not apply to us. We weren't sure what adultery was, but we figured it was something only adults could do. We certainly hadn't murdered anybody. We wouldn't think of taking God's name in vain (though we had heard a few other children do it). Our neighbors didn't have any cattle we could covet (even if we wanted to). Like many children, we both remember the commandment we most worried about breaking was "honor your father and your mother."

Perhaps you also grew up wondering how many of the commandments applied to your daily life as a child. Now that we are parents, we are thinking seriously about how we can teach our son the Ten Commandments (it's one of the promises we made at his Baptism).

We have been helped by turning to Martin Luther's explanations of the commandments in his *Small Catechism*. Luther helps us see that keeping the commandments involves more than merely avoiding certain behaviors. It is a matter of active Christian responsibility.

For example, Luther reminds us that keeping the commandment "you shall not take the name of the LORD your God in vain" means praising and thanking God as well as not cursing. Following the commandment "you shall not bear false witness against your neighbor" involves more than not lying about others. It means we will also speak kindly about them.

Luther's explanations reflect Jesus' teachings in the sermon on the mount. In Matthew 5, our Savior reminds us that anger can be a form of murder and that in God's eyes, lust is just as sinful as adultery. Jesus' words and Luther's explanations remind us that we all break God's commandments more than we like to admit. We may never have literally murdered anyone, but we have all been inappropriately angry. We may not make a habit of swearing, but none of us praises God as often as we ought.

As we teach the commandments to our children, we can help them to see that God's laws speak directly to their daily lives on the playground, at home, or at school. In all of these places, our children have opportunities to honor God and respect others. We can also discuss ways we can keep God's commandments more faithfully as a family, perhaps by working together to help a neighbor or by taking time for family Bible study.

Most important, we can help our children see that in one way or another, we all break God's commandments every single day. Yet "if we confess our sins [God] is faithful and just and will forgive our sins" (1 John 1:9). God's laws are not just for adults. Nor is God's grace. Thanks be to God, who showers unending mercy upon us all, young and old alike.

Teach me, Lord God,

as I teach my children about Your laws.
Show us new ways we can
faithfully keep Your commandments
and
honor Your holy name.
In Jesus' name. Amen.

God's Answer

Psalm 77:11–20

We were struggling to keep up with our writing deadlines and other daily tasks. Harold was working a full-time job while writing every night and on his one day off each week. Rochelle was taking care of Sam full-time and writing in the early morning and evening hours. All three of us were crabby because we spent so much time working and little time relaxing. We didn't have the money for professional childcare. Even if we did, we hadn't found a place that was quite right for our son. Our shoulders were weighed down with worry. We prayed for some relief, some small window of opportunity that would help us take care of our responsibilities.

One day, out of the blue, a friend offered to have Sam join her weekly play group. It would be free. It would give us an extra eight hours a week of uninterrupted writing time. We cheered! The next week, our neighbor approached Rochelle about doing a baby-sitting exchange. Another three hours of writing time appeared. We rejoiced! Now we would be able to meet our deadlines (and maybe even have some time to relax).

Some might say we are "lucky" people or the recipients of a wonderful coincidence. We knew otherwise. God was at work in our lives. God had lifted the worry from our shoulders. The psalmist said this about God: "Your path led through the sea, Your way through the mighty waters, though Your footprints were not seen" (Psalm 77:19).

We know God does not always speak to us from a thundercloud. God's answers to our prayers do not always come in neat little packages tied up with shiny bows. Sometimes God's answers aren't printed on a billboard but come to us in tiny, incidental ways. We don't always see that the coincidences in our lives may actually be God's answers to our prayers. We recently read an article that reminded us to be aware, to pay attention, lest we miss God's work in our lives. The answers we receive may not be what we expected or wanted. But that does not mean God is not listening. God hears all our prayers. And God responds to them in the way that is best for us.

During a time of difficulty, a friend prayed to God for help and guidance. A few weeks later an old friend called her, wanting to reconnect. As the two women began to catch up on the past 10 years, they discovered they had both faced similar health problems in recent years. Our friend said to us, "Her call, her presence in my life at this moment, was God's answer to my prayers."

Parenting is full of stresses. In the midst of those stresses, the best thing we can do is to lean on God every moment of every day. God invites us to cast our burdens upon Him and He works miracles with our lives. We may not always see God's footprints, but if we pay attention, we will notice our loving Savior's mighty mark on our lives.

God of miracles,
prompt me to pay attention
so I don't miss even one
of Your marvelous deeds.
In Jesus' name.

Amen.

Parade

Mark 11:1–10

Our son Sam attended his first parade at the age of 3. We stood with him beneath a shady tree on a hot Fourth of July morning, sweat rolling down our faces. Sam waved his miniature flag and giggled each time another band or float or fire engine passed. We joined the crowd in cheering as local celebrities rode by in convertibles. We felt ourselves caught up in the rhythm of the music as bands marched by playing patriotic tunes. And we all felt disappointed when the parade came to an end after an hour, much too soon for Sam.

"I like parades," Sam announced when we arrived home. For weeks he talked about trombones and bass drums, clowns and horses, and the man who threw candy to the crowds. He even created a parade of his own, composed of stuffed animals lined up in the living room. Although we've attended many parades through the years, we understood Sam's enthusiasm. Whether we're 3 or 73, there's something about a parade that brings a thrill to the heart.

The best-known parade in the Bible is the one a crowd of adoring onlookers threw for Jesus when He came into Jerusalem a few days before the Passover. Many Christians recreate this parade every year on Palm Sunday. We march around the church (or if the weather's nice, around the block), waving palm branches and shouting, "Hosanna to the Son of David!"

The first Palm Sunday was no doubt a thrilling occasion for those who greeted Jesus along the road into Jerusalem. Most people feel a rush of excitement from being part of a cheering crowd. Many of those acclaiming Jesus that day hoped He would become a great political leader and restore Israel to the glory it knew under the reign of King David. They worshipped

Him as a hero. Most of them could not have imagined that before the end of the week, this same Jesus would be crucified like a common criminal.

A large crowd also gathered at Jesus' trial before Pilate. Just five days after Jesus was greeted like a king, He stood humbly before Pilate while a mob shouted, "Crucify Him!" There is power in crowds. In the wrong circumstances, the same thrill we feel while watching a parade can become a surge of rage and hatred.

Each year, when we relive the events of Holy Week, we remember how fickle we humans can be. One moment we're praising Jesus, and the next moment we're betraying Him. When Jesus looked out at the crowd that greeted Him on that first Palm Sunday, He knew the events that lay ahead. He knew the fickleness of the crowd. Yet He did not condemn them or turn them away. Whether He was being worshiped or reviled, Jesus never stopped loving those He encountered.

Like that crowd in Jerusalem, we too may praise Jesus on Sunday only to turn around and deny Him during the week. Still, Jesus never stops loving us. Whether it's Palm Sunday, Good Friday, or somewhere in between, our Savior has mercy on us always.

Hear me, Lord Jesus,
when I praise You.
Forgive me, Lord,
when I deny You.
Help me, Lord,
to be more faithful.
Thank You, Lord,
for never failing me.
Amen.

Photo Moments

Romans 6:4–11

We call them "photo moments." We're doing something with our son, when suddenly he makes an irresistibly charming expression we want to remember forever. We get out the camera and start clicking away, hoping to capture the moment. Sometimes we get it. Sometimes we don't. We have albums full of photos that document our efforts.

Most parents have experienced their share of "photo moments." Often these moments seem to be over before we even realize they have begun. It's then that we realize how fleeting life's special moments can be. When our son was an infant, parents of older children often told us, "Enjoy him now. He won't be this age forever." We have enjoyed Sam at every age (well, there are a few moments when he was 3 we'd rather forget). Still, as we watch him grow, there are times we wish we could stop the clock.

It's so easy to forget what our children were like when they were first learning to crawl, then walk, and talk. Perhaps that's why so many people enjoy becoming grandparents. They get to relive the experience of watching a young life develop through all the ages of childhood.

"Photo moments" are almost always fleeting. Yet there is one moment in our life which remains forever new no matter how old we may become. On the day we were baptized, we were joined with God through the death and resurrection of Jesus. "We were therefore buried with Him through baptism into death in order that, just as Christ was raised from the dead through the glory of the Father, we too may live a new life" (Romans 6:4).

Our Baptism was no fleeting moment. It remains with us constantly, unaltered by the tarnishing affects of time. Because we have been baptized, every day of our life is a new day, bringing fresh opportunities to serve Christ. We can begin each day by repenting of our sins and rejoicing in the power of Christ within us.

Our physical bodies grow old. Wrinkles appear, gravity has its way with our bodies, and our bones become more fragile with each passing year. Although many have tried, we cannot ultimately stop the clock on the process of physical aging. Even so, with St. Paul we can proclaim that "we do not lose heart. Though outwardly we are wasting away, yet inwardly we are being renewed day by day" (2 Corinthians 4:16).

The next time you experience one of those "photo moments," remember your Baptism into Christ. Even when life's most pleasurable moments have passed, your relationship with Christ will continue, forever unfading.

Prayer idea:

Get out your camera and take a picture
of something or someone that reminds you
of God's love for you. As you snap the photo,
thank God for the blessing you are recording
on film. Don't forget to thank God again
when you get the photo developed!

Do You Believe?

Mark 9:14–24

A while ago we read about a survey reporting that almost 90 percent of Americans believe in God. Some people might claim this statistic shows that most people who live in the United States are religious. We don't think the survey reveals much of anything.

Almost 90 percent of Americans believe in God. So what! Most people also believe fast food is unhealthy and watching too much television is a waste of time. But how many of these people are willing to give up double cheeseburgers and their favorite TV shows?

Believing in God does not necessarily affect the way one lives. Believing in God may merely be an intellectual or sentimental position. It need have no more influence on one's life than believing the world is round or the Mona Lisa is a magnificent work of art.

We do not doubt that most people believe in God. What we wonder is this—how many of us believe God? That is a different matter altogether. The difference between believing in God and believing God is much like the difference between believing in love and believing you *are* loved. You can believe in love as a concept or a principle, and it need not affect your life at all. However, when you believe you *are* loved, your life gains new meaning. You live in a relationship with the one who loves you.

So it is when you believe God. When you believe God, your family and neighbors can see a difference in your life. They can see the effect God's love has upon you. Believing God means trusting God. It means trusting that God will keep all His promises.

As parents, we hope to be able to believe our children when

we ask them to tell us the truth. Whether we believe them often depends upon how trustworthy they have been in the past. We know we can believe God because God has proven trustworthy all throughout human history. God has never failed to keep a promise.

Even so, many of us struggle to believe God. Because we are weak, we all wrestle with doubts. Sometimes we wonder if God's promise of a new creation and everlasting life will ever come about. We may doubt God's promise to provide for all of our family's needs. We may struggle to believe that God walks with us through all the moments of parenting, especially when our children are acting up and our patience is wearing thin. Like the man who brought his demon-possessed son to be healed by Jesus, we may occasionally exclaim, "I do believe; help me overcome my unbelief!" (Mark 9:24).

Only by the help of the Holy Spirit can any of us believe God and trust His promises. When the Spirit works in our life, people will notice. It will make a difference. Do you believe God? Ask the Holy Spirit to help you overcome your unbelief.

Prayer idea:
Throughout the day, speak aloud the words recorded in **Mark 9:24** as a prayer.

The Good Ol' Days

Exodus 16:1–15

A friend of ours is the father of a precocious son who just started the second grade. Our friend's son doesn't like his new teacher and has been reluctant to head off to school each morning. One day, our friend asked his son what the matter was. "Oh, Dad," he replied, "I miss the good ol' days back in first grade. School just isn't what it used to be."

Most humans, young and old alike, tend to be nostalgic about certain parts of the past. Especially when we are making a transition to a new situation, we may long to return to the way our life used to be. We remember feeling this way shortly after our son was born. We had been married more than four years when our bundle of joy arrived. We had looked forward to his arrival and were thrilled to be parents. But there were days (and many nights) when we longed to return to our childless state. Remember what it felt like to sleep for an entire night without interruption? Remember how we used to decide at the last minute to go out for supper? It didn't take us half an hour to pack the car. Oh yes, those were the good ol' days, we would muse.

Of course, we were fooling ourselves. Our days before Sam arrived were not always happy. Many times we feared we would never slow down enough to have a child.

People who have recently moved or started a new job may experience a similar longing for the past. The best-known Bible story about misguided nostalgia is recorded in Exodus. When God freed the people of Israel from slavery in Egypt, He led them, under the leadership of Moses, through the Red Sea and on toward the Promised Land. After the Red Sea miracle, the people responded with joy (see Exodus 15:1–21). Just three days later, however, the Israelites started to grumble because of a lack of water. Soon they were actually longing to return to Egypt (Exodus 16:3). They reminisced about the good ol' days of slavery when they had plenty of food to eat. Certainly the Israelites were looking at their past through rose-colored glasses. In their nostalgic longing, they failed to trust that God would continue to provide for their needs in the present. As a result, God punished them and caused them to wander the wilderness for 40 years.

There's certainly nothing wrong with remembering the way life used to be. Sometimes, however, we sentimentalize our past. When we do that, we often fail to see the many ways God is providing for us in the present. Even in the best circumstances, the first months of parenthood are difficult. Career changes and new homes bring fresh challenges. Yet God has promised to encourage and guide us through all of the transitions of our lives. God brought us through the good ol' days and God still leads us now.

Prayer idea:

Remember a difficult time from your past
and reflect upon how God guided you through it.
Offer a word of acknowledgment to God
by praying,

"Thank You, Lord,

for leading me now just as You led me then."

Now Is Not Forever

Isaiah 40:25–31

It had been a horrible day. Even an optimist could agree it was a day that did not bear repeating. We began our morning with a stopped-up shower drain. After the first shower, the tub was full of cold, murky water and the rest of the family had to skip bathing. We tried to call the plumber, only to discover that our telephone was out of order. Then our son, working diligently on potty training, forgot to use the potty ... three times. Oops. But the day had to improve from there, right? Wrong.

Rochelle and Sam headed out for a stress-reducing walk. A few blocks away, they came across two gigantic dogs running loose. The dogs galloped toward them, barking all the way. Sam shrieked and clung to his mother, who bravely fought off the dogs until their owner appeared. Sam cried all the way home.

The rest of the day seemed to get worse with each passing minute. Maybe we *should* have stayed in bed. Upon reflection, we couldn't decide if the rest of the day was really that bad or if it just seemed so. Maybe the problem rested with our faulty vision or our "stinking thinking." Whatever the case, everything about our life that day seemed to stink.

It's at times like these that we need to remember that now is not forever and our forever is held in Jesus' hands. Sometimes, in the midst of difficulties, we universalize our distress. We start to believe everything in our life is as bad as this one problem we are encountering at the moment. We forget that God has blessed us every day in many ways. We lose sight of the fact that, even in this most difficult situation, God is holding us in His hands.

The prophet Isaiah reminds us: "He gives strength to the weary and increases the power of the weak. Even youths grow tired and weary, and young men stumble and fall; but those who hope in the LORD will renew their strength. They will soar on wings like eagles; they will run and not grow weary, they will walk and not be faint" (Isaiah 40:29–31).

For us, as Christians, our hope is always in Christ, in the knowledge that we have been forgiven and have received new life through Christ's death and resurrection. No matter how awful our day might be, no matter what anyone might say about us or to us, our status as children of God, loved and saved by Jesus, does not change. No matter what we encounter in this life, nothing can take that away from us.

Now is not forever and our forever is held in Jesus' hands. We live with a certain, everlasting hope. " 'No eye has seen, no ear has heard, no mind has conceived what God has prepared for those who love Him'—but God has revealed it to us by His Spirit" (1 Corinthians 2:9–10).

Blessed Jesus,

> when I feel trampled on and frustrated,
> focus my eyes upon You and Your promises.
> Uphold me with Your mighty hand.
> Amen.

Content

Philippians 4:10–13

Our friend's first child, our goddaughter, suffered from colic. Now, she is a happy and contented elementary school student. Back then, she was what we'd call "malcontent." Nothing seemed to soothe her. Being picked up irritated her, but being left in her crib made her scream loud enough for the neighbors to hear. She wanted to eat, but the food didn't calm her. She hated her wet, sticky diapers, but she wasn't happy with the clean ones either.

There were a few things that worked—for an hour at a time. Riding in her car seat. Being held while one of her parents pedaled the stationary bike. Being jostled just right as her parents walked her around the house while listening to the same Bach tune.

Our goddaughter could not resonate with Paul's claim, "I know what it is to be in need, and I know what it is to have plenty. I have learned the secret of being content in any and every situation, whether well fed or hungry, whether living in plenty or in want" (Philippians 4:12). But how many of us can? When we are together all the time, we want to be alone. When we are alone, we feel lonely. When we have plenty of work, we are stressed and exhausted. When we don't have any work, we question our worth. Our house isn't big enough; the kids, though healthy, aren't smart enough; and God didn't give us the looks we had hoped for. When will we ever be happy? What will it take to make us "content?"

Nothing. The truth is, no *thing* will do it for us. Getting a bigger house, a more delicate nose, and better behaved children won't prove our worth. It won't make us content. Trying to achieve contentment through our own or our children's accomplishments is a game everyone loses.

Paul tells us what did it for him. It wasn't a magic pill or material wealth. It was Christ. Paul proclaimed, "I can do everything through [Christ] who gives me strength" (Philippians 4:13). Take a deep breath and repeat those words to yourself. Do it 20 times today. Twenty times an hour if you need to.

The secret to Paul's contentment was Christ. Paul knew he was made right with God because of Christ's death and resurrection. Christ lived within him, reminding him that each situation he encountered did not have power over him. Christ worked within Paul to give him strength and helped him to remain content no matter how difficult situations became. (Remember Paul's life wasn't a trip on Easy Street. He was persecuted, imprisoned, shipwrecked, and plagued by a "thorn in the flesh.")

So here we are, almost 2000 years later, facing a pile of dirty dishes and unpaid bills, laundry strewn all over the floor, and perhaps a grumpy child to round out our day. We can survive these trials, even feel content in the midst of them, because we are not defined by our current situation. We are nourished by Jesus living within us. We are strengthened by Christ's promise to be with us always. We can be content, no matter what. Like Paul and those others who have gone in faith before us, we can do all things through Christ who strengthens us, just as He nurtured and sustained them.

Dearest Jesus, dwell within me.

Strengthen and uphold me so I can live each day with the confidence that only You can give. Amen.

A Season of Singing

Song of Songs 2:11–13; Psalm 30:11–12

It had been one of those days. Our 3-year-old son had been suddenly struck with the "grumpy virus." The clothes his mother had chosen for him to wear were *wrong*. "I want to wear my train shirt!" shouted Sam, throwing the other clothes in the air. Sam moped throughout the morning, uninterested in reading, coloring, or playing with his cars—activities he usually enjoyed. At lunch, Sam picked at his peanut butter and jelly sandwich, a meal that on most days he would devour in seconds. On it went, all day long. Living with Sam the grump was no fun at all, neither for him nor for us.

Just before bed, as Sam nibbled on a snack, he began to sing along to the tape playing in the kitchen. "Bless the Lord, oh my soul!" he crooned in perfect harmony. Sam knew the whole song by heart. His eyes shone like two little beacons of light as he serenaded us.

The Song of Songs talks about a season of singing. It says: "See! The winter is past; the rains are over and gone. Flowers appear on the earth; the season of singing has come, the cooing of doves is heard in our land" (Song of Songs 2:11–12). Spring comes to those of us who live in the north as a breath of fresh air, a beautiful thawing of all that has been frozen, and a resurrection of what appeared to be dead.

On Sam's day of moping, we were in need of a little spring ourselves. As parents, our lives can occasionally seem like a prolonged "Lenten season." We may become overly focused on all our failings and shortcomings. We might dwell upon what we lack in life, and lose sight of all the ways God has blessed us. We may begin to regard all we do for our children as a drudgery. We may care and provide for them out of duty and discipline—but without joy. Duty and discipline are not all bad. We need both. We also need to celebrate our children and our families. We need to rejoice in their presence in our lives.

Now, when things seem dark and gloomy at our house, when all of us are feeling grumpy and sulking, when we lose sight of God and the joy of life, we declare a season of singing. We listen to an inspirational tape and begin to sing along. If we feel up to it, we dance a bit. We let God remind us that the seasons of our lives include seasons of joy, singing, and dancing. For even on our "grumpy days," we live in the light of an empty tomb and look forward to that day when we will sing Christ's praises forever.

"You turned my wailing into dancing; You removed my sackcloth and clothed me with joy, that my heart may sing to You and not be silent. O LORD my God, I will give You thanks forever" (Psalm 30:11–12).

God of all seasons,
I dedicate my songs
and
my life to You.
In Jesus' name.
Amen.

Sin Is Not Like Snow

1 John 1:8–10

We woke up just a few days before Easter to a yard full of snow. Since we live in Wisconsin, spring snowfalls are nothing new to us. Over breakfast, Rochelle asked Harold why he seemed to be in no hurry to attend to the task of shoveling the sidewalk that leads to our house. "It's April," he replied. "If we wait a few hours, it will melt."

Harold was right, of course. Unless you live in a permafrost climate, snow will melt eventually—even in Wisconsin. But in this sin-filled world of ours, snow is just about the only problem that will finally disappear if you ignore it long enough.

If you're heading down the highway and you suddenly hear a rattling sound coming from beneath the hood of your car, most likely the sound will not stop until you open the hood and do something about it. If you step on the scale and discover that you are overweight, you can't plop down in front of the television and expect that the extra pounds will miraculously disappear while you sit there. If you say something hurtful during an argument with your children or spouse, simply pretending the incident never happened will not help. The hurt will remain as long as you do not confront it.

Sin affects our relationships both with God and with other people. Sin sticks to our souls like plaque clings to teeth. It remains an ever-present reality in our lives. Not a day goes by that we do not sin. When we sin, we disappoint God and cause harm to ourselves, to others, and to our world. One of the effects of sin is that it causes us to deny our very sinfulness. We overlook the wrong we do. We ignore or justify our hurtful behaviors. But sin is not like snow. If we ignore sin, it will not disappear on its own. It will continue to fester and infect our relationships.

Though we humans may ignore the affects of our sinful condition, God does not. God confronted the problem of human evil by sending our Savior to die for our sins. Jesus, who lived and loved without sin, died in our place on Calvary. When we look to the cross, we can ignore our sin no longer. When the Holy Spirit brings us face to face with God's mercy, we see that we don't need to overlook our problems any more. God's grace gives us the courage and the wisdom to face our sinful condition and to confront all the problems our sin brings upon us. God's grace (and only God's grace) melts away sin.

Are there problems in your life you've been afraid to confront? Turn to the One who can help you to work through them.

Dear Jesus,
sometimes I try to ignore problems
in my relationships with You,
> my family,
> or
> my friends.

Give me the courage to face those problems, knowing
that with Your help I can overcome them.
Amen.

The Greatest Gift

Matthew 6:19–21; Ephesians 2:8–10

Spring cleaning often brings surprises at our house. Recently, while rummaging through a dusty closet, we came across a shelf of boxes we forgot we had. We opened them to discover towels, tablecloths, a food processor, and a variety of household knickknacks—gifts from our wedding. We were married in 1991, so this stuff has been sitting around, unused, for quite awhile.

Most of us have received at least a few gifts that end up tucked away on a storage shelf somewhere. In time, we may forget all about them. Hopefully, we have also received some gifts we have treasured. These are usually gifts from significant people in our lives or presents that have special meanings attached to them. They may be practical gifts we use everyday or beautiful items we display prominently in our home.

The Bible teaches us that of all the gifts we have received, there is only One that will last forever—our Savior Jesus Christ. Through our Baptism into Christ, God has established a relationship with us that is far more valuable than any other gift we will ever receive. This relationship includes God's promise that He will forgive us daily, provide for all our needs, and bring us one day into life everlasting. Because God's gift lasts forever, we find ourselves perpetually unwrapping it, delighting each day in the treasure we discover.

When our children are baptized as infants, they receive the gift of Christ's love before they are fully able to understand what it is all about. As parents and baptismal sponsors, we promise to teach our children about this gift as they grow in years. We promise to tell them all about Jesus and how He lived, died, and rose again to establish an everlasting relationship with them. We promise to bring them to divine worship where they can join with us in thanking Jesus for all He has done for them. We promise to help them unwrap God's gift, to honor and cherish it every day of their lives. If these promises are neglected, we run the risk that our children's greatest gift may remain unopened and unacknowledged, as though it were some sort of unwanted present.

What are you and your children doing with the gift that matters most? Is your relationship with Christ tucked away in a remote part of your life? Or is it visible in your everyday words and actions for all the world to see?

Prayer idea:

Find your children's baptismal certificates
or other mementos from their baptism day.
Ask God to help you teach your children
to delight daily in the gift of their relationship
with Christ.

View from Above

Psalm 8

As the airplane ascended Sam stared out the window with his eyes open wide in amazement. "See down there. That's Milwaukee. That's where we live," said Harold.

"Where we live?" asked Sam.

"Yes, one of those houses down there is ours."

"Our house is big," said Sam, dumbfounded that from high in the sky, the world in which he lived looked so different. Could those matchbox-sized houses and those cars that looked like ants really be part of his neighborhood?

We have both taken a number of airplane rides in our lifetimes. Yet the view from above amazes us every time we see it. In our daily routines, we easily become self-absorbed, concerned primarily about matters that affect us and our immediate community. When we peer down at the world through an airplane window, however, our perspective broadens. We see rivers, mountains, and trees and marvel at God's creation. We see cars, houses, and city streets and realize that we are but a small part of a vast and varied world.

King David lived long before the time of air travel. Yet in Psalm 8, he conveyed a feeling similar to that which we experience whenever we look at God's world from an airplane. Perhaps David sat beneath a clear sky one night, stared up at the multitude of stars, and realized the vastness of God's creation. He wrote: "When I look at Your heavens, the work of Your fingers, the moon and the stars that You have established; what are human beings that You are mindful of them, mortals that You care for them?" (Psalm 8:3–4 NRSV).

David's words remind us of a wonder too marvelous for any of us to comprehend. The same God who created and continues to sustain this incredible universe also cares for each of us as though He has nothing else to do. God created billions of intricate stars, yet God notices each hair on our head (Matthew 10:30). The same God who made mountains and forged rivers gives breath to the tiniest child.

Sometimes, we humans become blinded by our own self-centeredness. Caught up in the daily tasks of parenting, we can easily lose sight of the "view from above." We can become overwhelmed by details—washing, cleaning, cooking, shopping. We race from one task to the next. After a while, we may fail to see the needs of those who live beyond our life's familiar boundaries.

But God is different. God sees everything—the "big picture" and every little part of it. God sees the smallest flower, hears the softest whisper, and touches all creation with grace beyond our imagining. No wonder David proclaimed, "O LORD, our Lord, how majestic is Your name in all the earth!" (Psalm 8:1).

Prayer idea:

Join your voice with King David's and read **Psalm 8** aloud as a prayer of praise to God.

High and Low

Psalm 139:1–10

It was a high point in our lives. Quite literally and in many other ways too. The three of us sat together, soaring above the clouds in a DC-10 airliner, on our way to Vermont where we would spend a week with Harold's parents. Sam bounced up and down in his seat, chattering as he stared out the window. He kept informing the other passengers, "We're flying in an airplane."

We turned and smiled at each other, delighted to see our 3-year-old son enjoying himself. "How wonderful to be together and enjoy ourselves," said Harold.

"It's one of those moments when life seems perfect," replied Rochelle.

We held hands, nibbled on peanuts, and discussed our vacation plans. As we peeked out the window at the cotton ball clouds and miles of beautiful blue sky, we both felt grateful for all our blessings.

King David wrote about our Creator: "Where can I go from Your Spirit? Where can I flee from Your presence? If I go up to the heavens You are there" (Psalm 139:7–8).

Literally sailing among the clouds, we remembered the words of the psalmist and felt God's power and presence. God is always with us, smiling upon us in life's "sky high" moments.

Yet in this life none of us remains among the clouds forever. As we made our descent, the plane hit a pocket of turbulence. The aircraft rattled. Sam stopped his chattering. He gripped the arm of his seat. His face turned an ashen color.

"Oh no," moaned Rochelle. "Sam, are you going to be sick?"

Sam nodded. We frantically searched for a bag to catch the inevitable mess to come. (Where are those things when you need them?!) We signaled for the flight attendant, who arrived … a few seconds too late.

We scrambled to clean up the mess, which covered Sam as well as most of our carry-on luggage. Suddenly, we did not feel so grateful. "This is a disaster," groaned Harold.

As the putrid odor spread throughout the aircraft, we feared the wrath of other passengers. Instead, we received sympathy and much needed help. The flight attendant mopped up around us and handed us towels while several passengers comforted Sam. "Happened to me once," said a middle-aged man. Sam had become the center of attention, encircled by the compassion of strangers.

We hadn't planned to begin our vacation this way. Yet as we reflected on the incident, we realized God was just as close to us in that dreadful moment as He had been when we were soaring above the clouds.

King David went on to write: "if I make my bed in the depths, You are there" (Psalm 139:8). Even in life's most undesirable experiences, God is with us, giving us strength and providing the help we need. We cannot escape God's loving embrace, no matter how high or low we go.

Dear Jesus,
wherever I go
and
whatever I do today,
never let me forget that You are always by my side.
Amen.

Keys of the Kingdom

Matthew 16:13–19

There are few moments so terrifying for parents, or so exhilarating for teenagers, as the day Mom and Dad first hand their teen the key to the family car. Most often, it is no simple process. First, the teenager must endure a lengthy lecture about being responsible, driving the speed limit, and being home at a reasonable hour.

The teenager stands there, bobbing up and down impatiently. "Yeah Mom. Yeah Dad. I've heard all this before. Now can I have the key?"

Reluctantly, the parent hands over the key and watches out the window. The lead-footed teenager squeals out of the driveway, missing the mailbox by mere inches.

Most of us adults have been driving so long we take for granted the privilege of possessing a car key. Some of us own so many keys we hardly think about them—unless, of course, they're missing.

Keys are symbols of trust. We do not hand our car keys over to our teenage children until we trust them to drive safely. We would never leave the keys to our homes with someone we know to be dishonest. When Jesus told Peter, "I will give you the keys of the kingdom of heaven" (Matthew 16:19), He was entrusting him with a sacred responsibility.

Martin Luther understood the "keys of the kingdom of heaven" to refer to the privilege and responsibility of Christian forgiveness. Christ gave these keys not only to Peter but also to the whole Christian Church. Christ has entrusted us with the task of forgiving one another.

We know we can trust God to forgive our sins when we repent because He first forgave us when Jesus died on the cross. We can trust God to keep His promise that we will receive everlasting life through our Savior Jesus Christ. Our God is trustworthy. God also wants us to be worthy of trust.

God trusts us to forgive, not to bear grudges. God trusts us to share the Gospel with our children, friends, and neighbors by witnessing our faith and through the way we live. "Get rid of all bitterness, rage and anger, brawling and slander, along with every form of malice. Be kind and compassionate to one another, forgiving each other, just as in Christ God forgave you" (Ephesians 4:31–32). The next time you reach for a key, remember the most important key you possess is the one Christ has given you.

Prayer idea:

Every time you touch a key today,
ask Jesus to help you forgive others
as He has first forgiven you.

Our Very Best Friend

John 15:9–17

Imagine that you have a friend who lives in your neighborhood. Sometimes, she stops by your home or calls you every day, usually when she's struggling with some sort of problem. She talks for hours, though she rarely asks for your advice. You listen to her patiently. In fact, when she calls, you drop whatever you're doing just to give her your attention.

She seems to appreciate your friendship. What's strange, however, is that when your friend's situation starts to improve, you rarely hear from her. You can go days, even weeks, without hearing from her.

What's stranger still is that whenever you want to talk to this friend, she never has time for you. She never returns your phone calls. She never reads the letters or e-mails you send to her. When you finally meet up with her and start to tell her about something important, you can see she's not listening.

Unfortunately, we sometimes act just like this friend in our relationship with Jesus. We fall into the habit of talking to Him only when we need something. When our lives are going well, we may avoid Jesus. Though He is always attentive whenever we call out for help, we don't always take the time to listen to what our Lord has to say to us through His Word.

When Jesus was transfigured high on a mountain, God's voice proclaimed from a cloud, "This is my Son, whom I love. Listen to Him!" (Mark 9:7). Jesus continues to speak to us today through the Scriptures and through the proclamation of His Word. When we fail to take time to regularly delve into the Bible, worship, and pray, we shut ourselves off from what Christ has to say to us.

One day our son came home singing a song he learned in Sunday school. "Oh, Jesus is my Friend," he chanted. Jesus is, of course, our Savior, the One who died and rose again that we might be reconciled with God and live eternally. As Sam is learning, Jesus is also our Friend, the One who walks with us through every moment of our life on earth. Jesus is our very best Friend, who would do anything for us, even give His life to save us.

One of our tasks as Christian parents is to help our children see that Jesus is also their best Friend. When we read the Bible, pray, and attend worship as a family, we are taking time to listen to what our Friend has to say to us. So we ask ourselves: what kind of friends are we to Jesus? Do we share all the moments of our lives with Him or do we talk to Him only when we need something? Do we listen to what He has to say? And what kind of example are we giving to our children? Do they know how to treat their very best Friend?

Dear Jesus,

I confess that I am not always
a reliable and faithful friend to You.
Yet despite all the times I've let You down,
You have never once abandoned me.
Thank You, Jesus, for dying for me.
Thank You for being my very best Friend.
Amen.

"It Must Be Here Somewhere!"

Luke 15:8–10

Rochelle was staffing the church nursery. Sam brought her a toy drum, held up his two index fingers, and said, "Where are the 'ones'?"

"The what?" asked Rochelle.

"The 'ones'!" Sam said louder, using his fingers to imitate a drummer.

"Ah! You mean drumsticks!" said Rochelle. "Let's look."

Rochelle led Sam and his friend Joey to the big toy box where they began to look for the drumsticks.

"They must be here somewhere," muttered Joey as he and Sam threw toys out of the box one at a time. They searched with a fervor that would please a rescue team. When the drumsticks didn't turn up in the toy box, they combed every inch of the nursery. And wouldn't you know, in the corner of the room, stuck behind a baby doll in a carriage, rested one lone drumstick.

"We found it!" shouted Joey jumping up and down. By his side, Sam danced, clapping and cheering, "Hooray!"

In Luke's Gospel, Jesus tells a story about a woman losing one of her 10 silver coins. Jesus says, "Does she not light a lamp, sweep the house and search carefully until she finds it? And when she finds it, she calls her friends and neighbors together and says, "Rejoice with me; I have found my lost coin." In the same way, I tell you, there is rejoicing in the presence of the angels of God over one sinner who repents" (Luke 15:8b–10). This parable tells us that to God, every one of us is precious. When one of us repents, no matter who we are to the world, the angels rejoice.

Sometimes we experience moments in our lives when we

feel less valuable than other people. It is not always easy to see that God loves *us*, especially when we fail to live as we ought. We lose our temper with our children. We forget to pray before we fall asleep. We lose our way as parents—no longer able to discern whether what we are doing for our children is right. Ever aware of our failures, inside our hearts an aching voice may start to wonder, "How could God really love a rotten parent like me?"

This parable reminds us that we are *so* valuable to God that our Savior would carefully search for us and then rejoice when we are found. Despite what the world or others might say about us (or our parenting), God always cherishes us. And when we turn to God, when we look to God for comfort and hope, then God and the angels rejoice.

The best way to remind ourselves of our value, of God's love for us, is to keep soaking ourselves in God's loving words and presence. We go to church. We receive the Lord's Supper. We are reminded of God's enduring love as we hear the words, "Given and shed for you." We pray each day. We read of God's merciful acts and compassionate deeds in the Bible. And we thank God for finding us when we were lost. We thank God for cherishing us more than we could ever imagine.

God of all compassion,
You have searched for me
and rejoiced in finding me.
I know You love me
and find me valuable.
In Jesus' name.
Amen.

Questions, Questions

Mark 12:18–34

Most children love to ask questions. As a parent, you will no doubt encounter a variety of questions in the years ahead. Some of them may be manipulative ("Why can't I eat a cookie now?"), but many will simply be the result of curiosity ("What happens when we die?"). For most children, asking questions is a natural process through which they learn about themselves and their world.

One of our tasks as parents involves taking the time to answer our children's questions with love and respect, especially in matters of our Christian faith. When we don't know the answers, we can turn to the Bible or our pastor for guidance. Yet it is important to honor every question and seek to answer it, no matter how trivial it may seem. By doing so, we convey to our children that we value our Christian faith and want to help them grow deeper in their relationship with Christ.

During His time on earth, Jesus answered a lot of questions. His responses didn't always satisfy His listeners. When a rich ruler asked Jesus, "What must I do to inherit eternal life?" (Luke 18:18), the ruler hoped to hear he would be saved because he tried to obey all the commandments. When Jesus declared that he must give all his possessions to the poor, the man "became very sad, because he was a man of great wealth" (Luke 18:23).

On some occasions, those who questioned Jesus were seeking to trap Him or undermine His authority. When the Pharisees approached Jesus with a question about paying taxes to Caesar, they came with a hidden agenda (see Matthew 22:15–22). They wanted to manipulate Him into responding in a way that might result in trouble with the Roman authorities.

Jesus saw through their evil intent. He answered their question and sent them away shaking their heads in amazement.

Many of Jesus' questioners were sincerely seeking answers. Nicodemus the Pharisee seemed truly baffled when Jesus explained to him that one must be born again to enter the kingdom of God. "How can this be?" Nicodemus asked (John 3:9). Jesus' answer enlightened not only Nicodemus but all who seek God's salvation (John 3:16).

Like those who approached Jesus in biblical days, we too come to Jesus looking for answers. He never sends us away empty. Jesus sees through our manipulative questions and listens compassionately to the sincere ones. We might not always receive the response we want, but in one way or another Jesus will tell us exactly what we need to know. Jesus said, "Ask and it will be given to you; seek and you will find" (Matthew 7:7).

Jesus,

grant me both wisdom
and
compassion as I seek to answer
my children's many questions.

Thank You for patiently listening to me
when I am confused
and
for guiding me by Your Word
and
the power of the Holy Spirit. Amen.

Still More Questions

Luke 20:1–8; Luke 10:25–37

A few years ago, our son passed through a stage where he would indicate what he wanted by asking questions. When Sam was hungry, he would suddenly appear with a jar of peanut butter in his hand and ask, "Does Mommy want to eat now?" Or Sam would put on his jacket, grab his father's hand, and head toward the door shouting, "Does Daddy want to go outside?"

To improve Sam's communication skills, we started responding to his inquiries with questions of our own. "Sam, do *you* want to eat now? Do *you* want to go outside?" Our questions forced Sam to think about his own needs and desires and take more responsibility for his actions.

As we study God's Word, we are amazed at the vast number of questions that appear in the Bible. Jesus lived on this earth long before the advent of the game show "Jeopardy," but He certainly knew how to phrase His answers in the form of a question. Many times, when people came to Him searching for answers, He would send them away with a question of His own. Jesus' questions forced His listeners to examine their own lives and consider the motives behind the questions they asked.

When a lawyer approached Jesus asking, "Who is my neighbor?" (Luke 10:29), Jesus told him the parable of the good Samaritan. Jesus ended his parable with a question Christians have pondered for 2000 years: "Which ... do you think was a neighbor to the man who fell into the hands of robbers?"(Luke 10:36)

The lawyer answered correctly that the traveler who cared for the injured man was his neighbor.

"Jesus told him, 'Go and do likewise'"(Luke 10:37).

Jesus knows the power of a question to shatter our pretenses and dig to the heart of life's matters. Consider the following questions (which are just a few of the many Jesus asked) as you examine your own walk with Christ:

"And can any of you by worrying add a single hour to your span of life?" (Matthew 6:27 NRSV).

"Why do you see the speck in your neighbor's eye, but do not notice the log in your own eye?" (Matthew 7:3 NRSV).

"Where is your faith?" (Luke 8:25).

"I am the resurrection and the life. Those who believe in Me, even though they die, will live, and everyone who lives and believes in Me will never die. Do you believe this?" (John 11:25–26 NRSV).

And perhaps the most important question of all—the one Jesus asked His disciples, and the one we all must answer eventually: "Who do you say I am?" (Matthew 16:15).

Dear Jesus,

give me the courage
to examine my life in the light of Your Word.
Amen.

Show and Tell

Colossians 3:15–17

"Bye Mom. See ya."

"Aren't you going to give me a good-bye hug before you head off to school?"

"Uh … not today, Mom. Gotta go."

"Wait a minute! What do you have in your hands?"

"Uh … oh you mean this box? Oh, I can't lie to you, Mom. Slinky's in the box. I wanted to take him to school."

"Why do want to take your pet chameleon to school, David?"

"For show and tell. Can I please? It would be so cool ..."

"Why don't you just tell your classmates about Slinky? I don't think they actually need to meet him."

"Ah, Mom. It's not the same hearing about something when you don't get to see it."

If you are the parent of elementary school-age children, "show and tell" might be a part of your routine as well. A friend of ours reports that every time another household item is missing, she suspects it will probably turn up at her son's school.

The concept of "show and tell" is basic. Children show an interesting or valuable object to their classmates as they tell them all about it. We like to think of Christian evangelism as a form of "show and tell." We can tell others all about our faith in Christ, but unless we show them what Jesus means to us, our testimony comes up a bit shallow.

St. Paul wrote, "And whatever you do, whether in word or deed, do it all in the name of the Lord Jesus" (Colossians 3:17). As we live out our faith and share Christ's love with others, our deeds need to complement our words. As our friend's son said, "It's not the same hearing about something when you don't get to see it."

As Christian parents, we serve as evangelists to our children. When they are baptized, we promise to teach them all about Jesus. Keeping that promise is a matter of showing as well as telling. If we implore our children not to smoke while indulging ourselves with cigarettes, our words will sound insincere. If we ask our children to make Christ their first priority when our own primary affections lie elsewhere, they will see our hypocrisy.

"Show and tell" faith cannot be accomplished on our own. We all come up short in the "showing" department occasionally. That is why we draw comfort in knowing that Jesus is the master of "show and tell." Jesus didn't just tell us He loves us. He showed it. Jesus revealed the truth of His words by His death on the cross. He gave His life so even when we fail to show Him our love, we can still be certain that He loves us, and that He will forever.

Dear Jesus,
help me to show my children that I love them
and
that I love You.
Amen.

Everything for Jesus

Colossians 3:23–24

When we first learned we were going to become parents, we spent many hours discussing what parenthood would be like. Like many naive first-time parents, we focused primarily upon the grand and glorious moments we would experience. We imagined birthday parties, graduations, and cheering for our child at sporting events or academic ventures. We envisioned family time at the breakfast table and cuddly moments at bedtime.

Now that we are "seasoned" at child raising, we look back on our pre-parenthood naiveté and laugh. Like all parents, we have discovered that much of parenting is just plain hard work. There is little that is grand or glorious about changing diapers, washing clothes, or nursing a sick child back to health. In our pre-parenthood years, we never realized how exhausted we could feel at the end of a day.

We are delighted to be parents. We have experienced more wondrous moments than we could have ever imagined. But we no longer fool ourselves. There is nothing glamorous about this job.

Still, every aspect of parenting is important. Cleaning up vomit, removing week-old candy bars from pants pockets, and repairing broken toys may not be particularly appealing activities. Yet we all know these unglamorous tasks are as much a part of parenthood as "cuddle time" and goodnight kisses.

St. Paul recorded words that could become the motto of all parents. He wrote, "Whatever you do, work at it with all your heart, as working for the Lord" (Colossians 3:23). Paul reminds us that everything we do, no matter how menial or unappealing it may seem, provides us with an opportunity to serve Christ.

Often we equate service to God with traditional activities like volunteering, tithing, or singing in our church choir. Serving Christ, however, extends far beyond what we do at church on Sunday morning. Every moment we breathe provides us with another opportunity to glorify the One who gives us all that we have and are. It may not be immediately apparent that changing a dirty diaper is a way of serving Christ and glorifying God. Yet when we realize that all our life belongs to God, we start to see that every kind deed we do, even if it seems small or unglamorous, is part of our Christian calling.

Jesus said, "Whoever can be trusted with very little can also be trusted with much" (Luke 16:10). Remember that the next time you're involved in one of those unappealing parental tasks. Ask Christ to guide you so whatever you do, you will do it with all your heart, and you will do it for the Lord.

Dearest Jesus,
inspire me to put my **whole heart** into all my tasks today.
Let all I do be done for You.
Amen.

"Thank You ... You're Welcome"

1 Thessalonians 5:16–18

For weeks our son had worked diligently at learning his manners. He mastered "I'm sorry" early (no doubt because of a few too many "timeout" moments). "Please" was a no-brainer since Sam quickly learned that unless he spoke it, he would not receive what he wanted. "Thank you" and "you're welcome" baffled Sam for quite a while, however. Sam knew to say "thank you" when he received something. He just wasn't sure what to say when he gave.

One day Harold asked Sam to bring him his shoes.

Eager to help, Sam raced to the closet and returned holding his father's loafers. As he handed them to Harold with a huge smile on his face, Sam shouted, "Thank you, Daddy."

"Oops, Sam," Harold replied, "I'm the one who says, 'Thank you.' Then *you* say, 'You're welcome.' "

"Thank you, Daddy," Sam said again. "Now you say, 'You're welcome.' "

"No, no, Sam. You say, 'You're welcome.' "

The conversation continued like a comedy routine, until eventually Harold realized that maybe Sam was actually getting it right. Whenever we asked Sam to do something for us, he almost always responded to our requests with joy. He seemed genuinely pleased to be able to help his parents. It was as though he was saying, "Thank you for giving me the honor of being able to help you."

As Christians, we can utter a similar sentiment to God as we go about our daily lives of serving Christ and helping others. We know God has given us everything we have and are, including our very lives. We wake each morning to a day full of opportunities to say "thank You" to God for all our blessings.

As we head off to work, we can say, "Thank You, God." Thank You for my body and mind which I use to make a living.

As we change diapers, prepare school lunches, or wash dirty clothes, we can say, "Thank You, God." Thank You for the gift of my children and the joy they bring to my life.

As we sit in traffic, stand in line, or endure the obnoxious behavior of others we can say, "Thank You, God." Thank You for sending your Son to die for the world's sins. Thank You for raising Him again so even when life on earth is difficult, I am sustained by the joy of my Savior's presence and the knowledge that one day I will live with You forever.

We add, "Thank you Sam." Thank you for reminding us that every moment we live and give is an opportunity to express our gratitude to the One who blessed us with life in the first place.

Prayer idea:

As you go about your daily tasks today,
thank Jesus for the many opportunities
He gives you to serve Him and help others.

What's Happening?

Isaiah 55:6–13

We were sitting with friends at a church conference banquet. The banquet program had been going on for quite some time and all of us felt a little restless. At a table behind us, a little girl—no more than 3—wiggled through most of the program. At one point, the band began to play a loud musical introduction, over and over again—a cue for a tardy speaker. Unable to see, the 3-year-old stood on her chair, perched herself on the tip of her toes, and said loudly, "What's happening?" We all chuckled, knowing that we were wondering the same thing (but were too grown-up to say it).

What's happening? It's a fair question. This past year, a 10-year-old boy from our neighborhood died at school from a brain aneurysm. Stunned by this tragedy, parents and teachers gathered to wonder aloud, "What's happening?" We discussed how we would care for this child's family and how we should explain the death to our own children. We wondered how to go on in a world where children can go to school and not come home. Our conversations led to other tragedies: car accidents, school shootings, fires.

We were saddened that so many children cannot count on reaching adulthood. That night, we looked at our own child with a little more tenderness, a little more love, knowing that we too could be struck with an unexplainable tragedy. We held on tightly as we hugged Sam good night, trying to savor that little boy smell, just in case it might be our last chance.

Many nights we stumble into bed, weary of the world we encounter during the daylight hours. We pray our nightly prayers, asking God to embrace all those who hurt, even those who are nameless to us. We thank God for our blessings. Then we settle down to sleep, restless as it may be, struggling with issues beyond our human understanding. As we do, we feel a bit like that little girl standing on tiptoe trying to peer above the crowd and wondering all the while, "What's happening?"

Through the prophet Isaiah, God spoke words that speak to us in moments when we wrestle with the hurts and mysteries of this world. "'For my thoughts are not your thoughts, neither are your ways My ways,' declares the LORD. 'As the heavens are higher than the earth, so are My ways higher than your ways and My thoughts than your thoughts'" (Isaiah 55:8–9).

Isaiah reminds us that like a little girl on tiptoe, we humans are too small to see or fully comprehend what God is doing in the grand scheme of the universe. We may question why God doesn't do something to stop all the suffering in our world. God's answer is not the one we necessarily want to hear—"My ways are not your ways." Still, it is an answer we need to learn to live with. All the while, we trust that ultimately God knows what is best. We trust that one day, through our Lord Jesus Christ, God will remove all the sin and suffering which prevent us from seeing clearly.

In the meantime, we who wonder "what's happening" cling to Isaiah's promise: "those who hope in the LORD will renew their strength" (Isaiah 40:31). These words don't take the pain of loss away. Death doesn't hurt any less. But these words do remind us that God will see us through all the troubles we face.

Creator God,

    strengthen me
    in the face of events I cannot understand.
    Lead me
    to hope in You.
    Walk with me.
    In Jesus' name.
    Amen.

Only Jesus

John 6:35–69

"I'm hungry!" shouts Sam as he makes his way down the stairs for breakfast.

"How about a bowl of oatmeal?" asks his mother.

"NO! Cookies!" shouts Sam. "Chocolate cookies!"

"Toast?" offers his mother.

"Pizza for breakfast! Pickles and pretzels!" shouts Sam.

"Oatmeal or toast. That's your choice," says Rochelle.

"Cookies!" repeats Sam.

We may know we are hungry. We may even think we know what we hunger for. But do we know what is best for us? Do we know what will best satisfy our hunger and nourish our bodies? Most of us experience physical hunger about three times a day—sometimes more. We also encounter a different kind of hunger each day—spiritual hunger.

When we experience physical hunger, our stomachs growl, our brains fail to compute, and we begin to whine and moan. When our souls become empty, when our spirits are hungry, we experience similar symptoms. We may yell at the kids more than we want. We may lash out at our spouses or ourselves. We feel slightly uncomfortable, slightly off, like something is not right. We know we need something ... but do we know what will satisfy the hunger within us?

Most of us know, intellectually, that we cannot fill the spiritual hole within us with just anything. Still many of us try. Food, sex, drugs, alcohol, achievement, physical beauty, material success—all are ways we seek to nourish our starving souls. These fillers might bring temporary satisfaction, but like a candy bar on an empty stomach, the high is short-lived. Very soon the satisfaction drops like plummeting blood sugar, and we are left feeling worse than before. We are more hungry, more anxious, more desperate than ever. We know our need but we don't always know the right answer.

Jesus does. In John's Gospel, Jesus speaks of Himself as the One who fulfills our spiritual needs. Jesus says, "I am the bread of life. Whoever comes to Me will never be hungry, and whoever believes in Me will never be thirsty" (John 6:35 NRSV).

Jesus told His hearers that He is the bread that satisfies. He is the One who gives eternal life. This teaching terrified and angered many who heard it. Jesus talked about Himself as food—and not ordinary food, but food that would make them live forever. Many could not bear this and left.

Jesus asked the 12 disciples if they too wished to leave. Peter responded, "Lord, to whom shall we go? You have the words of eternal life. We believe and know that You are the Holy One of God" (John 6:68–69).

Jesus is the bread that fills the aching hunger within our souls. He nourishes us each day as we pray. He invites us to His table and feeds us with the Meal of His own body and blood. He fortifies us in church and at home as we hear and read the Bible. Jesus is the only one who can provide us with the food our soul needs. Jesus can satisfy our spiritual hunger. Only Jesus. Jesus is the food we've been waiting and hoping for. Jesus.

Lord Jesus, to whom shall I go?

You have the words of eternal life.
You alone can satisfy my deepest longing.

Amen.

A Letter to Samuel (On the Occasion of His Second Birth)

Galatians 4:3–7

Dear Samuel,

We sure do you love you. But we'll be honest. As your parents, we need all the help we can get. So today we are doing something for you that is more important than opening a million-dollar bank account or making sure you get into Harvard. Today we are bringing you to worship at church. We will stand around the baptismal font. The pastor will sprinkle your head with water, but God is the One who will be doing all the work. Today you will become one of God's born again children.

Dear Samuel, we hate to admit it, but in the future we will sometimes fail to love you as we ought. We cannot be available to support you every moment of your life. But God is your perfect heavenly Father. God promises to be present for you always through all that lies ahead.

That is why we are also making promises today. We are promising to do our best to teach you about the One who will always be your Best Friend. We are promising to bring you to worship week after week to worship your Savior.

Now, we imagine that when you are 2, you may not be keen on sitting through the service. Why, you might even try to outshout the pastor. You will squiggle and wiggle and grow bored like all children do. Yet even if you don't quite understand what worship is all about, we know your heavenly Father will be pleased to see you in His house of prayer.

And when you are a teenager, you might just look us in the eyes and announce quite boldly that you're not coming to church anymore. We are not sure what we will do if that happens. We hope we will be patient with you. But we might not be. We won't always know the right words to say to you. Still, we will draw comfort from knowing you are baptized and therefore you have a Parent who is more patient and wiser than us.

And one day, Samuel (many years from now, we hope), you will come to a place of worship to pray and watch as your earthly parents are laid to rest. We imagine that moment will hurt you. No longer will we be here on this earth to comfort you and laugh with you. Yet we will leave this earth with the knowledge that you still have a perfect Parent who will guide you and love you long after we are gone. And you will let go of us, knowing that because we are all children of the same heavenly Father, you will see us again.

Samuel Moffitt, you are God's very own child. From this day forth, God will never leave you. Sometimes in the years ahead, you will run from God. Other times you will run to Him. Yet through it all, God will be there for you. Forever, Samuel Moffitt. Forever.

Heavenly Father,

I entrust my children into Your care,
knowing that even when I fail them,
You will always love them perfectly.
In Your Son's name.

Amen.

"Helper Girl"

Psalm 116:12–19

"Do you want to come over and play?" Rochelle asked the neighbor girl. She is four years older than our son, but still enjoys playing with him from time to time.

"I can't," she replied. "I'm a helper girl today."

"What's a helper girl?" Rochelle asked.

"I help my parents. Whatever they ask, I try to do. Unless it's too hard or grown up."

Helper girl. What a great idea. One of the lessons we try to teach our son is the importance of helping others. At home, we have taught him to take responsibility for tossing his own trash, picking up his toys, putting his clothes in the hamper. He doesn't always understand the lesson or follow through on his tasks, but we're trying. We will introduce him to offering envelopes soon and then to serving at church and helping others in need. We want our son to understand that helping is a concrete way he can say "thank You" to God.

The writer of Psalm 116 asked, "How can I repay the LORD for all His goodness to me?" (Psalm 116:12). God created us and called us to be His children. God sent Jesus to die for our sins that we might have new life through Him. Jesus gave us the gifts of Holy Baptism and the Lord's Supper that we might experience God's grace in tangible ways. We have received so much. Why wouldn't we want to show our thanks to God by helping others however we can?

St. Paul reminds us that "those able to help others" play a major role in Christ's Church, alongside teachers, healers, and miracle-workers (1 Corinthians 12:28). Helping is one of those spiritual gifts that knows no age limit. What would it be like if we went through life as God's "helper girls" and "helper guys"? We've tried it, and it bears recommending.

When we focus on helping, we don't pass by another shopper who has dropped her packages. We pick them up. We smile. We wish her a blessed day. When we're driving, we don't lay on the horn or rush through yellow lights. We let the man with just a few items go in front of us and our loaded cart at the grocery store. We offer free baby-sitting for our friends. We help an elderly neighbor with her household chores. And at the end of the day, we have received so much from helping, from sharing little bits of God's love with others, that our hearts are overflowing with joy.

Helping reminds us that we are blessed to be a blessing. We are gifted to share our gifts. We are helped by Christ so we might help others in return.

Jesus my Helper,

> show me new ways that I may help others
> and thereby reflect Your love.
> Amen.

Shoes: A Parable

Isaiah 52:7–10

"How beautiful on the mountains are the feet of those who bring good news" (Isaiah 52:7a).

The week before Thanksgiving, Mary's doctor diagnosed the pain in her fingers as rheumatoid arthritis. The ailment couldn't have struck at a more inopportune time. In a few days, Mary's four children, their spouses, and all eight of her grandchildren would come for their annual holiday visit.

As Mary prepared for their arrival, the arthritis dampened her spirits. Household tasks she once accomplished with ease became difficult chores and painful reminders of her ailment.

Despite the pain, Mary managed to prepare a feast that would feed the entire family. By the time everyone arrived, her fingers throbbed.

Mary tried to shake her sullen mood. But as she raced about the house attending to last minute details, she tripped over a small pair of shoes that had been left in the entryway by one of her grandchildren.

Mary picked herself off the floor, unhurt. She glanced about and saw that she was surrounded by almost a dozen pairs of shoes, scattered haphazardly near the door. *What a mess,* she thought. All at once, a whole host of negative thoughts rushed through her mind.

"O Lord," she prayed, "why do You burden me so? I cook and clean and no one lifts a hand to help me. And those children toss their shoes and toys around the house with no concern for others."

As Mary continued to prepare the meal, she counted the days until everyone would return home and leave her alone in her misery. She started to take the roast from the oven when she felt a small child brushing against her knee.

"Hi Grandma."

"Not now," Mary snapped. "I'm busy."

"But Grandma," the child replied, "I want to tell you something."

"You'll have to wait."

"But Grandma ..." the child persisted. Then she spoke in the softest of voices. "I just wanted to say I love you."

Mary peered down at her granddaughter, still brushing against her knee. Then she looked again at all those shoes that had annoyed her just minutes before. Suddenly Mary lifted up her granddaughter and despite the pain in her fingers, she held the girl close as they danced and twirled about the kitchen.

"Grandma, what are you doing?" the girl asked in amazement.

"It's those shoes," Mary explained. "I just realized that each pair belongs to somebody I love. How sad I would feel if even just one pair of them were missing."

Consider this: Like the shoes at Mary's house, might some of your burdens actually be blessings?

Prayer idea:

Look at pairs of your children's shoes and thank God for the gift of the ones who wear them.

Morning's Mercies

Lamentations 3:22–24; Psalm 121

Before our son was born, sleep came to us as a daily gift from God, a chance to renew and refresh our bodies and spirits. We crawled into bed each night and prayed our thanks to God before slipping off to dreamland. The first few months with Sam changed those nights forever. It wasn't just that he was waking every three hours to eat. A switch had been thrown, something inside us had permanently changed. We slept like the night sentry, with one eye and one ear open, always ready to defend our child.

Shortly after the long nights of feeding ended, Sam began attending a play group. Then began a stretch of time we called "illness overtime." Week after week, Sam came down with something that required us to be cleaning or cuddling him throughout the night. It seemed like he would never get well.

Now we are in the stage of night terrors. Almost every night, Sam wakes up shrieking and crying (and consequently wakes the two of us). We are hoping that as our son grows older, we may again be able to make it through an entire night without being roused from our slumber. Probably not. One day he will be a teenager who wants to stay out with friends long after we have gone to bed. No doubt, we will sleep with one ear open, waiting to hear his familiar footsteps on the porch so we can know he is safe from harm.

On many of the nights when Sam was an infant, we would wake to care for him and then be unable to sleep again. We would watch the clock. We would sit by the window and wait for the city to wake up, thankful each time a light appeared in a neighbor's home, reminding us that we were not alone. Sometimes we would sip tea or pray. Too often we worried.

Would we be able to function the next day? How would we manage on so little sleep?

On those dark and lonely nights, times that return even now, we held onto the promise God makes: "Because of the LORD's great love we are not consumed, for His compassions never fail. They are new every morning; great is Your faithfulness" (Lamentations 3:22–23). We survived each night, knowing that the One who neither slumbers nor sleeps (Psalm 121:3–4) watched by our side, caring for and loving our son. In addition, we knew morning would bring still more gifts from God, new compassions, God's bright shining mercy to guide us through the day.

Trusting in God's mercy as we wait for the new day seems like such a small thing. But when we wander through the dark—whether it is a long dark night or the darkness of depression or suffering—the light at the end of the tunnel brings hope. God's faithfulness shines for us in that light. It reminds us that night will end and morning will come. Every day. Every single day. Until the final day—when the deepest darkness of all will give way to the light of Christ's everlasting life.

God of **darkness** and light,
in the middle of the night,
remind me that You are with me;
help me to rest
in the promise of each new morning.
In Jesus' name.
Amen.

Stubborn!

"No! No! No! Noooooooo!" shouted Sam. "I don't like it! I don't want to go upstairs."

Bedtime. A few minutes earlier, Sam had been sitting at his little table, with a book in his hand. His eyelids would flutter, his head would tip forward, and the book would start to slip from his fingers. Just as he was in danger of falling over, Sam would catch himself and sit up straight, awake for a second or two. Then the whole process would begin again. Finally, Rochelle tapped him on the shoulder and said "Time for bed, Sweetie." With that, Sam jumped from his chair—wide awake—and began his temper tantrum.

The more we prodded Sam toward bed, the louder Sam screamed. We suggested. Sam screamed. We encouraged. Sam screamed louder. We shouted. Sam screamed and kicked and flailed his arms. *Temper Tantrum, Level 9; all hands on deck!*

Our family and friends assured us that 3-year-olds tend to act like this. Plus, he's human. And as a human, Sam desires one thing: his way. The more we ask him to turn from his way, the more desirable *his way* seems to be.

Sam is really not so different from the rest of us. We, too, want life to go our way. We tend to kick and scream (or pout) when life does not cooperate. When someone points out the error of our ways (or even gently encourages us to follow a new direction), we dig our heels into the ground and shout, "No!"

The people of Israel had the same problem. Speaking for God, the prophet Hosea wrote, "But the more I called Israel, the further they went from me" (Hosea 11:2a). The people of Israel were stubborn. Plain and simply, they wanted to have things their own way.

The prophet Ezekiel reported God's word to him about Israel's stubborn nature: "the house of Israel is not willing to listen to you because they are not willing to listen to me, for the whole house of Israel is hardened and obstinate" (Ezekiel 3:7). God did not turn away from these difficult people. Instead, God became creative. God promised to make Ezekiel as "unyielding and hardened" (Ezekiel 3:8) as the people of Israel were. God sent Ezekiel back to the people to try again. God continued to send prophets to the people of Israel until finally He sent Jesus—the One who would save all of us from our sin of rebelling against God.

All of us struggle with the desire to live by our own rules, with our own hopes at the forefront. When we are confronted with God's will, many of us respond like Sam reacted to bedtime: "No!" Thankfully, God does not leave us standing in the middle of the living room, acting like stubborn fools. God does not abandon us to our sins. In fact, God is even more stubborn than we are!

In our Savior Jesus Christ, God promises to love and provide for us, and God steadfastly refuses to abandon that promise no matter how much we resist. When we turn away, God pursues us until we are again reconciled. Jesus comes to us with open arms, welcoming us with unconditional, unrelenting mercy. Try though we may, we cannot be more stubborn than God.

Jesus, forgiving One, do not leave me.

Even when I turn from you,
I need to feel you near me.
When I am stubborn, stick with me.

Prod me and push me.
Hold me in Your arms.
Amen.

More than Enough

2 Kings 4:42–44

We had gathered to participate in a "hunger event," a practical lesson about how the world's resources are divided. After a time of prayer and singing, the leaders divided us into groups, each one representing a different continent of the world. Each group received a simple lunch of rice and beans according to their socio-economic status. Those of us assigned to the United States and Canada were given a plentiful serving of rice and beans and individual cans of soda, more than enough to sustain us through the afternoon. Those of us assigned to the third world countries received enough for each person to eat a spoonful of either rice or beans and drink a sip of water. This paltry lunch didn't even begin to quench our hunger and thirst. After we ate, we discussed what it means to have "enough."

In the United States, many of us think we need more than we have: more clothes, electronic gadgets, food, toys, and space. Advertising encourages both children and adults to "hunger and thirst" for more stuff. It tells us that without the most classy stuff, we lack what we need to be happy. The quest to acquire more material possessions has resulted in the emergence of an entire storage industry. When we don't have enough space in our home, we move to a bigger house or build extra rooms. We hire consultants to help us figure out how to organize our belongings. We buy fancy plastic containers to store our stuff. And when we still have too much, we rent storage space to hold it. Even with all this stuff, many of us still feel we need more.

The writer of 2 Kings tells us that the prophet Elisha once fed one hundred people. Elisha's servant didn't believe there would be enough food to go around. " 'Just give it to them,'

Elisha replied. 'The LORD has promised there will be more than enough' " (2 Kings 4:43b CEV). More than enough. We don't hear that very often. No one comes on television and announces, "You have more than enough."

This story about Elisha reminds us that whenever we are lacking something we truly need, God will take care of us. When we look back on our lives, at the times when we have worried about having sufficient money, space, or possessions, we can see that God was true to His promises. We may not have always received exactly what we thought we needed, but somehow God always provided for us (though we may not have seen it at the time).

A friend of ours recently left his job because it was the right thing to do. He didn't have another. He had some savings and the promise of a place to live for a few months. Our friend trusted that, regardless of what happened, God would provide for all his needs. On that day and many since, our friend's faith has reminded us that God keeps promises. We can be certain that no matter what troubles life brings us, God will take care of us. The same One who sent His Son to save us, who has promised us life everlasting, has also promised to provide for all our daily needs in our life here on earth. God always gives us "more than enough."

Gracious God,

You have filled my life
with more than enough blessings to sustain me.
Free me from needing to have more "stuff."
Instead, let me rest my soul in You.
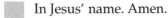
In Jesus' name. Amen.

The Magic Word

2 Corinthians 12:7–10

"What's the magic word?" we used to ask Sam when we were first teaching him manners.

"Pleeease," he would reply, catching on quickly.

Sam became a polite little boy. However, we soon learned that referring to "please" as the "magic word" was a big mistake. Sam literally believed the word contained a special power that could be used to manipulate others. All Sam needed to do was add that little word to any request and it would produce whatever he wanted. Or so he thought.

"Pleeease, Mom, may I have some candy?"

"Not before supper."

"I said please!"

"The answer is no."

"But I said please! I said the magic word."

Sam continued to plead to no avail. He was learning one of life's most difficult lessons. Sometimes, no matter how earnestly or politely we ask, we will not receive what we want.

As parents, we may deny our children's requests because we want to do what is best for them. Three-year-old Sam was unable to understand that candy before supper was not in his own best interest. As Christians, we are grateful that God is watching out for our welfare. That doesn't stop us from occasionally asking for something we want even when we don't need it.

Sometimes, we Christians think that if we only ask God in the right way, if we plead with enough earnestness, then we will receive exactly what we ask for. Just as Sam regarded "please" as a magic word, we may think of prayer as a magic act. Thankfully, prayer doesn't work that way.

God invites us to ask for our needs (see Philippians 4:6). That doesn't mean we will automatically receive everything for which we ask. God knows what is best for us, even when we don't. And God promises to provide us with exactly what we need.

St. Paul knew this to be true. In his second letter to the Corinthians, he describes a mysterious ailment which he referred to as "a thorn in my flesh" (2 Corinthians 12:7). Paul wrote that he "pleaded" with God three times to take away this affliction. Paul probably used the word "please" a few times. But God did not remove Paul's ailment. God said, "My grace is sufficient for you, for My power is made perfect in weakness" (2 Corinthians 12:9).

Paul learned to accept his "thorn in the flesh." He came to see that, for reasons beyond our understanding, God sometimes denies our requests. With Paul we say, "Thank You, God" for not giving in to our manipulative ways.

Thank You, gracious God,

>   for always providing me with what I need
>   even when it's not what I want.
>   In Jesus' name. Amen.

Whom Do You Love More—
Jesus or Your Family?

Matthew 10:34–39

Jesus once told His disciples, "Do not think that I have come to bring peace to the earth. ... For I have come to set a man against his father, and a daughter against her mother, and a daughter-in-law against her mother-in-law; and one's foes will be members of one's own household" (Matthew 10:34–36 NRSV).

This is not the kind of Bible passage you would expect to hear in church on Mother's Day or Father's Day! Jesus spoke many words that challenged His listeners, and this speech is certainly among them. Jesus reminds us of a profound truth that we would sometimes rather not hear.

In this speech, Jesus went on to say, "Whoever loves father or mother more than Me is not worthy of Me; and whoever loves son or daughter more than Me is not worthy of Me. Those who find their life will lose it, and those who lose their life for My sake will find it" (Matthew 10:37, 39 NRSV). Here Jesus gets to the heart of His message. He calls us to follow Him, putting Him before everything and everyone else—even those people we love the most. Even our children. Even our parents.

For Jesus provides for us in a way that no one else can. Only Jesus can give us eternal life. Only Jesus' love lasts forever. All our other relationships on this earth will come to an end one day. No matter how close we may be to our loved ones, one day our relationship with them will be severed by death. It's not something we like to think about. Yet it is an undeniable fact. When we die, our loved ones will not be able to save us. Only Jesus can raise us from death. So it only makes sense that our relationship with Him becomes our foremost priority.

Of course, because we are sinful and selfish, putting Jesus first creates conflict. None of us gets our priorities right all the time. When we do put Jesus first, conflict often results. That is what Jesus meant when He said, "I have come to set a man against his father, and a daughter against her mother." Jesus' words are *descriptive* not *prescriptive*.

Jesus isn't telling us we should try to pick fights with our children. He is simply describing what can happen when He becomes our top priority. If we put Jesus before all others, including our family, sometimes our loved ones will object. Sometimes the result will be conflict. "Mom, why do you always make us go to church?" "Oh, Dad, I don't want to say my prayers." "Why do you give our money to the church when you could use it to buy me a new bicycle?"

Perhaps you have heard a few comments like these. Your relationship with Jesus should not destroy your other relationships, but sometimes it will cause difficulties. In a world where many people are vying for your attention, following Jesus and living the way He calls us to is not easy.

Thankfully, He forgives us when we fail and gives us courage when conflicts arise. Through it all, our Savior holds before us His never failing promise that one day He will welcome us into the joy of life everlasting.

Holy Jesus,

> I want to love You most of all.
> Grant me the courage and faithfulness to do so.

> Amen.

Jesus Uv Me

Jeremiah 1:4–10

While Rochelle attended a meeting, Harold was given one task for the evening—to put 3-year-old Sam to bed. But since Harold was suffering from the flu, this task would not be easy. One moment Harold was shivering and wrapping himself in a blanket. The next moment he felt so hot he thought he would pass out. This misery was accompanied by waves of nausea and an uncontrollable cough. Sam, however, seemed to feel no pity for his father. In fact, he was having a bad night of his own.

When bedtime arrived, Samuel resisted as usual. After much persuasion, Harold convinced him to lie down. At this point, Harold was feeling so nauseated that the room was spinning before his eyes. "Good night, Sam," he said, and started to leave the room.

Immediately Sam let out a piercing scream, followed by that kind of obnoxious whining sound only a 3-year-old can make. The sound reverberated through Harold's head, through every inch of his aching body.

Harold responded with a shout of his own. He said some of those things every soon-to-be parent vows they'll never say to their kids. But his shouting only caused Sam to increase his volume.

Sam was saying something, over and over. But Harold couldn't make it out. Sam was difficult to understand anyway, and he'd now become so hysterical, that his words just sounded like gibberish. All the while Harold's headache grew worse.

Sam kept shrieking, repeating the same phrase again and again, until finally Harold began to understand what he was saying. "Jesus uv me ... Jesus uv me," Sam shouted.

Jesus loves me. Of course. Sam wanted his father to sing the song that was part of his nightly ritual. Harold had felt so sick, so tired, he had neglected to take time for Sam's usual bedtime prayers, hoping Sam wouldn't notice if he skipped them for just one night.

Harold sat on the floor next to Sam's bed. With a hoarse voice, he croaked out the words Sam knew by heart—"Jesus loves me this I know, for the Bible tells me so."

Immediately Sam's crying ceased, and he settled comfortably into bed. A moment or two passed. The next thing Harold remembers is sitting on the floor next to Sam's bed with his head on the mattress near Sam's stomach. Sam was touching his father's hair lightly with his hand, something he had liked to do ever since he was a baby. Sam's eyes were closed, and he was speaking softly, "Yes, Jesus uv me. Yes, Jesus uv me. Yes, Jesus uv me. The Biboo tell me so."

Despite his nausea, Harold felt strangely calm. In his illness, he was being ministered to by a 3-year-old. And he wondered—is God speaking to me through this child?

In the Bible, the boy Jeremiah protested that he was too young when God called him to become a prophet. But God told him, "Do not say, 'I am only a child.' ... I have put my words in your mouth" (Jeremiah 1:7, 9). We know that God speaks to us through Word and Sacrament, but can God speak through a child? You bet! Our God can do anything!

Gracious God,

as You ministered through the young prophet
Jeremiah,
minister through me and through my children.
May the words we speak bring glory to You.
In Jesus' name.
Amen.

"What Are We Going to Do?"

John 14:1–14

Early in the morning, around the time the sun begins to rise, our son tumbles into our room, climbs onto the bed, and snuggles in between us. The first question out of his mouth is usually, "What are we going to do today?"

Now that he is 4, Sam has a fairly good grasp of the schedule. He knows that every Sunday he goes to church. On Mondays he spends the day with his friend Elijah. Tuesdays are shopping days. Still, like any good ritual, he must ask every day. He then ventures his best guess, "Shall we go to the library today?" Once he knows the plan, he begins to speculate on the activity. What books will he read? Will he and Elijah play outside? Will he be able to buy his favorite cereal?

There's something in all of us that longs to know the future. More than knowing what the day will hold, we long to be certain that all will be well. We've heard many cancer patients say they could endure the pain better if they only knew they would be getting better, if they could magically see into the future and glimpse a happy outcome.

As Christians, we know God has provided us with all we need as we venture on our journey through this life. We have God's Word, the gifts of Baptism, and the community of the Church. We have weekly worship and the Lord's Supper. We are able to pray and share with God our fears about what lies ahead. Still, we sometimes long for something more, for a magical telescope that will peer into the future and tell us when to expect hard times.

Jesus' disciples longed for their own peek into the future (and maybe a map to guide them on their journey). Jesus had been talking about going and preparing a place for them in his "Father's house" (John 14:2). He said, "And if I go and prepare a place for you, I will come back and take you to be with Me that you may also be where I am. You know the way to the place where I am going" (John 14:3–4).

Thomas said to Jesus, "Lord, we don't know where You are going, so how can we know the way?" (John 14:5). Jesus told Thomas and the others, "I am the way and the truth and the life. No one comes to the Father except through me" (John 14:6).

Jesus reminded the disciples that although they did not understand the details, they did know the big picture: Jesus. As they trusted in Jesus and followed Him, He would lead them on their way.

Jesus' words provide a comforting answer to our anxiety about the future. As we follow Jesus and cling to Him, we need not be frightened about a road we cannot see. Sometimes, on long car trips at night, we will find a truck with bright taillights and settle in behind it. That truck becomes our beacon, a light to guide us through the darkest nights. Jesus is the "Light of the world" who leads us through the darkness on the road of life.

We all face uncertain futures. Not one of us knows what each new day will bring. But as Christians, we have the comfort of knowing that when tomorrow comes, we will be clinging to our dearest Friend.

> ## Jesus, You are the way,
> ### the truth,
> ### and
> ### the life.
>
> Be near me and guide me.
> > Hold my hand and lead me where You
> > would have me go.
> > Amen.

The Unchanging One

Psalm 119:89–91

"It must be difficult raising children these days." We have heard this comment many times. Perhaps you have too. We often hear these words from well-meaning friends (who are not parents) or from people of older generations. On one level, we generally agree with them. Raising children in the 21st century is no easy task.

We live in a society where no community is totally protected from random acts of violence. Many parents fear for their children's safety, even in settings traditionally considered to be secure, like schools and churches. With a few easy clicks, modern technology gives anyone access to pornography, violent music, and the diatribes of hate groups. It's no wonder many parents feel worried and paranoid.

In many ways, the world is a different place than it was just a generation ago. We were reminded of this fact when, at the age of 4, our son asked, "Mommy, did you check the e-mail today?" A word which did not even exist a few years before had become a regular part of our preschooler's vocabulary.

Of course, all change is not bad. The same technology that makes pornography so accessible can also become a powerful tool for proclaiming God's Word to a hungry world. Our children have access to learning opportunities that previous generations could not have even imagined. Advances in science and medicine mean longer, healthier lives for all of us.

On another level, the world really has not changed all that much. Since Adam and Eve turned their backs on God, generation after generation have lived in bondage to sin. Violence, injustice, and sexual immorality are nothing new. Just read through the Bible. Raising children has *never* been easy. Imagine the grief David felt when he mourned for his rebel son,

Absalom (2 Samuel 19:1–4). No doubt, many parents feared for their children's future when the Israelites toiled in slavery in Egypt and even more so as they made the tumultuous journey through the desert on the way to the Promised Land. Then there is the slaughter of the innocents by King Herod described in the gospel of Matthew: "Rachel weeping for her children and refusing to be comforted, because they are no more" (Matthew 2:18). What could be more horrible than that?

Anyone who's ever been a parent has worried about their children. And for all parents, the ultimate source of comfort remains the same throughout all generations. To an ever-changing world God says, "I the LORD do not change" (Malachi 3:6).

Because of human disobedience to God's commands, life on planet earth has never been easy. But in the end, the instability caused by violence and evil will not have the final word. Christ has conquered the power of death and the devil. "Jesus Christ is the same yesterday and today and forever" (Hebrews 13:8).

"It must be difficult raising children these days."

"Yes it is. Just as it has always been," we reply. "That's why we're teaching our child about Jesus. That's why we're clinging to the One who has promised He'll never change."

God of all times,
>
> I cling to You.
> Teach me
> and guide me.
> In Jesus' name.
> Amen.

Choices, Choices

1 Peter 2:9–10

It was supposed to be a quick stop at the convenience store to pick up a few necessities. "May I please can I have a candy bar, please?" Sam asked in a voice so sweet we knew just this once we'd have to say, "Yes."

"Only one. You can choose," Harold replied.

"Hooray," Sam shouted, as he surveyed the many shelves of sweets near the checkout counter. He reached for his favorite chocolate bar, but then suddenly saw another treat that looked equally enticing. He picked up that one, then put it down and reached for something else.

"You need to decide," said Harold, the impatient father. But the more Sam looked, the more confused he became. There were chocolate bars with peanuts and some with almonds and others with no nuts at all; some were filled with caramel and others with nougat. Another whole shelf contained other treats like licorice sticks and gum.

Sam lives with the privilege of fretting over which candy bar to buy, while children in other parts of this world have absolutely nothing to eat. Indeed, some observers have noted that many people living in the United States today suffer anxiety because they have too many choices placed before them.

The anxiety many of us feel about choosing a car, a home, or a career can be a symptom of an even deeper problem. Even with all the possibilities that lie before us and all the material goods we have to distract us, many of us suffer a deep emptiness inside ourselves. An old folktale tells of God talking to one of the angels about how humans were created. God says, "I made each person with a hole inside, a space so unique that only I can fill it."

Jesus said, "I am the bread of life. Whoever comes to Me

will never be hungry, and whoever believes in Me will never be thirsty" (John 6:35 NRSV). Jesus was talking about that hole deep inside us that only He can fill. Of all the choices and possibilities that lie before us, there is only one choice that can satisfy our most essential need—to know we are loved, forgiven, and cared for by the One who watches over all.

Jesus Christ is that choice. And ironically, it is not a choice we make. It is a choice God makes for us. God chose to come to earth in the person of Jesus Christ to die for our sins and rise again so we may have life everlasting. The Bible says that we did not choose God, but that God chose us—to be His people and to know all the blessings only Christ can give.

As a parent, you face many choices every day. Even when you make inappropriate decisions, you can draw comfort from knowing you have been chosen by Jesus. That hole deep inside you has already been filled. You need only hear Christ's call to experience all the blessings our Savior gives.

Dear Jesus,

calm my anxiety

about the choices I make each day—

that affect both my family and myself.
You have chosen me;

I have nothing to fear.
Amen.

What a Mess!

Deuteronomy 8:10–18

We had recently become authors and were feeling quite proud of our accomplishment. Now the day we'd been anticipating for months had finally arrived. We were headed to one of our first big book readings at a local bookstore. The store was about a half-hour drive from our house, so we needed to leave a little early. We had planned the schedule with military-like precision, including our son's visit to the home of friends.

We worked together in the kitchen, discussing the reading, while we made supper. Our son played in the back room. As Harold opened the oven to take out our meal, Sam entered the room with the unmistakable demeanor of a child who would soon be sick. He pressed his greenish-gray face against his mother's side and said, "I'm going to throw up."

Immediately, we discarded our perfect schedule. Suddenly, we faced a new dilemma—how could we honor our professional obligations and also care for our son? In his condition, Sam couldn't go to his friend's house, and we seemed to have no hope of finding a baby-sitter for a *sick* child on such short notice. The next hours unfolded chaotically as we frantically called sitters, cradled and cleaned up after our son, gulped down dinner, showered, and dressed.

Fifteen minutes before we were slated to go, we sat dressed and ready, proud of ourselves for overcoming our crisis. Just as the baby-sitter rang the bell, Sam got sick again—all over himself and the carpet. There we stood, just an hour before our big reading, with a literal mess on our hands. Harold scrubbed the floor. Rochelle, in high heels and a dress, carefully cleaned Sam. As we drove away from the house 20 minutes later, we said, "Someday we'll laugh about this!" And indeed, we have.

No matter what successes might come to us, no matter what we earn, achieve, or acquire, we must not forget that through it all we are guided by God. Sam taught us that by literally vomiting on our pride. Sam's stomach virus reminded us that life is about much more than getting ahead. Even when we do succeed (or barely make it through), we need to give credit where credit is due.

In Deuteronomy, the people of Israel were reminded that they would not get to the Promised Land on their own steam. Their journey and all their accomplishments came because of God. "You may say to yourself, 'My power and the strength of my hands have produced this wealth for me.' But remember, the LORD Your God, for it is He who gives You the ability to produce wealth, and so confirms His covenant, which He swore to your forefathers, as it is today" (Deuteronomy 8:17–18).

We can all remember this lesson. Everything we have and all we achieve come to us as gifts from God. As we pray, read our Bible, come to the Lord's Table, and worship at church, we are reminded that we are not free agents on this earth. We belong to God. Our lives are not our own to do with as we please. Through Jesus Christ, God has redeemed us, claimed us, blessed us, and promised to guide us as we journey through this life. All we achieve along the way are credits—not to us—but to God. "The human mind plans the way, but the LORD directs the steps" (Proverbs 16:9 NRSV).

Gracious God,

You are the One who gives me all my abilities.
You bless me and guide me
through both the great
and the gritty moments of life.
In Jesus' name I thank You.
Amen.

"The Worst Parent in the World"

Romans 7:15–25

Outside of church, we see one of our friends engaged in a battle that she would rather we not witness. She is hunched over the back seat of her car trying to extract her strong-willed 4-year-old daughter from the vehicle. The girl is clutching the seat belt with all her might while shouting, "No! No! I don't want to go to Sunday school."

Our friend is growing visibly angry, almost on the verge of tears. Later, after church, she confesses to us, "Sometimes parenting just brings out the worst in me." Then she asks, "Do you ever get frustrated?"

Yes, we confess, we often do. Frustrated with our son. But also frustrated with ourselves. And then we started talking. Really talking.

"Every morning when I wake up, I tell myself that today I won't get angry. Today I won't lose my cool. Then something happens. My daughter sasses back at me. She refuses to listen to me. I love my daughter, and I'd never intentionally do anything to hurt her. But some days I just want to scream. And then I feel like I must be the worst parent in the world."

"You're not alone," we say. "And you're not the worst parent in the world."

St. Paul was not a parent, but he described well the predicament many parents face when he wrote: "I do not understand what I do. For what I want to do I do not do, but what I hate I do" (Romans 7:15). Paul was describing human bondage to sin, the fact that no amount of good intentions can make us right with God.

Most Christian parents have good intentions. Ideally, we want to love our children, provide for all their needs, and help them in times of trouble. But in the real-life nitty-gritty world of parenting, ideals often fall by the wayside. All parents experience moments when their children fuss, whine, and act like belligerent fools. Our patience wears thin. We lose our temper. We say things we later regret. Sometimes, parenting brings out the worst in us.

Parenthood is a marvelous gift from God. Yet like all earthly institutions, it is marred by the power of sin. In those moments when we say and do things that are not helpful for us or our children, all we can do is fall on the grace of God.

We can confess our sins, both to God and to our children. We can also help our children to see the error of their ways (no, it is not right to provoke your parents). Then, together with them and enabled by the Holy Spirit, we cling to the mercy of the One who loves us even when we are at our worst. Again St. Paul said it well: "Who will rescue me from this body of death? Thanks be to God—through Jesus Christ our Lord!" (Romans 7:24b–25a).

Thank You, God,
for standing by me "for better and for worse."

Give me the patience and compassion I need
to become a more loving parent.
When I fail, reassure me of Your mercy
through Jesus Christ my Lord.
In His name. Amen.

Praying Myself to Sleep

Psalm 63

A few years ago, the doctor asked Rochelle, "Do you exercise?"

"If you mean, do I get up and put on special clothes and run around the block or jump up and down in front of the television—no, I don't. On the other hand, if you mean, do I run up and down two flights of stairs innumerable times each day to sort, wash, dry, fold, and put away laundry, not to mention the other gazillion times I make the same trip because I am chasing a 2-year-old—then yes, I do exercise," answered Rochelle. (Even worshiping with a preschooler can sometimes be a form of aerobic exercise.)

More times than we can count, friends have asked Rochelle, "When are you going back to work?" Back to work? She *is* working! She takes care of our son full-time. Part-time, in the wee hours of the morning and night, she writes. And every so often, she goes off for a day to speak to a women's group.

The complaint Rochelle hears most often from the women she speaks to is this: "I don't have time to connect with God!" In fact, many of them, busy taking care of family (and working as well), fall into bed each night too exhausted to pray. One friend, a working mother, reports having trouble staying awake while she helps her children say their prayers.

Both fathers and mothers struggle to find time to connect with God. We make sure our children eat and have clean clothes to wear. But talking to God falls into the same category as taking care of ourselves. We often do it only when it is an emergency. Just as we may go to see the dentist only when our toothache becomes unbearable, so may we also delay calling out to God until the situation becomes "9-1-1 urgent."

In Psalm 63, the psalmist expresses a yearning for God's company: "O God, You are my God, earnestly I seek You; my soul thirsts for You, my body longs for You, in a dry and weary land where there is no water" (Psalm 63:1). Those of us too busy to pray live in that dry and weary land. We constantly thirst for a taste of the living God. We need to make regular rest stops at the well of His Word, sacrament, and worship to fill up. That timeout with Him provides great benefit.

We once heard a Christian speaker suggest that busy mothers and fathers could also take "mini-retreats." By that, the speaker meant taking one- to five-minute breathers midday. She encouraged stepping outside or sitting down, taking several deep breaths, and praying. She suggested reading a psalm or simply asking for God's presence and blessing.

On those days when even a brief "timeout" with God seems impossible, you can still connect with God as you work. Pray for your family members as you fold their clean clothes. Pray for other drivers as you run your daily "limousine service" for your children. Sing a familiar hymn as you wash dishes. These moments are not nearly enough time with God for regular nourishment, but it beats going thirsty.

Calling out to God as we work can remind us that even when we feel disconnected, God is always connected to us. We are baptized and redeemed Christians—loved by God and saved by Jesus' death and resurrection. No matter how hectic our days may be, we will always belong to Christ. Remembering that makes each day's work a little less stressful.

Prayer idea:

Pray Psalm 63:1.

Ask God to fill your soul with living water.

Spiritual Food

John 6:22–27

"Hurry! We're late."

It was one of those moments which reminded us that parents never seem to have enough time. The alarm had failed to ring and all of us had overslept. Sam had a doctor's appointment across town and we had a number of important errands to do on the way.

As we rushed around the house, our little family looked like we were performing in our own slapstick comedy.

"Make sure Sam is dressed," said Rochelle.

"I can only find one of his shoes," replied Harold.

"I'm hungry," said Sam.

"Make Sam some toast," said Harold.

"Where's the checkbook?" asked Rochelle.

At one point all three of us collided in the kitchen.

"Ow," said Sam, as he picked himself up off the floor.

"Watch out," said Harold.

"There's a shoe behind the refrigerator," said Rochelle.

We all emerged from the mishap unscathed and continued rushing about in three separate directions. In a matter of 10 minutes we managed to get everybody dressed, comb our hair, find the checkbook, and make three pieces of toast.

Soon we were all in the car, headed across town, beginning yet another busy day.

"I'm hungry," said Sam, from the back seat.

"Didn't you eat your toast?" asked Rochelle.

"It's behind the fijerator," replied Sam. (At our house, it seems that everything eventually ends up behind the refrigerator.)

In our rush, we had managed to feed ourselves but had forgotten to make sure Sam had eaten.

"What kind of parents are we?" we both wondered aloud.

All parents occasionally experience moments like the one we just described. (You do, don't you? Please tell us we are not alone!) Fortunately, we manage to make sure our son eats a nutritious breakfast most mornings. We would consider ourselves negligent parents if we did not attend to our son's basic daily physical needs.

Parents who fail to feed their children are liable to be charged with child abuse. Yet we often overlook the fact that many parents are guilty of starving their children *spiritually*. Jesus said, "Do not work for food that spoils, but for food that endures to eternal life, which the Son of Man will give you" (John 6:27). Just as nutritious food strengthens our physical bodies, Jesus gives the spiritual nourishment we need to survive. When we gather at worship, receive the Lord's Supper, and take time to pray and reflect on God's Word, we are partaking of "spiritual food."

If we do not take time to pray with our children every day or to teach them about Jesus, we allow them to go hungry. Even the most devoted parents are tempted to "skip a spiritual meal" occasionally. We may think, *we don't have time to say grace,* or *I'm not feeling well; let's skip our bedtime prayers.* When we give in to those temptations, we risk beginning a pattern of ignoring our children's spiritual needs.

Remember to eat your spiritual food! And don't forget to make sure your children receive the food only Christ provides.

Dear Jesus,

You and Your love are all I hunger for.
Feed me and my family
with the food You alone can give.
Amen.

Cloudy Days

Exodus 17:1–7

For eight consecutive days, our fair city had been shrouded in clouds. Such weather is typical at the end of February. Of course, at the age of 4, our son did not yet know this. As we stepped outside to be greeted by yet another dreary day, he asked, "Where is the sun? Why has it gone away?"

We explained that the sun had not disappeared permanently, and that in fact it still existed. "No," replied Sam. "I think it has gone on a trip."

Many people battle depression during the winter months when it appears that "the sun has gone on a trip." As Christians, we also sometimes suffer from periods of melancholy when it may seem that "the Son has gone away." In moments of illness or stress, we may call out to our Savior, asking Him to be near us. It may seem in those moments that He is nowhere to be found.

As the people of Israel traveled through the wilderness on their way to the Promised Land, they experienced many moments when they doubted God was truly leading them. When they became hungry or thirsty, the Israelites started to complain to Moses. They forgot all that God had done for them in the past, how He had led them out of Egypt and through the Red Sea. They tested God saying, "Is the Lord among us or not?" (Exodus 17:7).

Of course, God was with the Israelites at all times, although they sometimes doubted and weren't always aware of His presence. In the same way, Christ is always with us, just as He promised He would be (Matthew 28:20). But like the sun on a cloudy day, our Savior's presence may not always be obvious to us.

The sun doesn't cease to exist just because sometimes we don't see it. Even on the dreariest days of winter, when the clouds lay thick and heavy, we know the sun's out there somewhere. We know we'll see it again. We would be foolish if we stopped believing the sun exists because we cannot always see it.

It is just as ridiculous to think Christ is no longer present simply because some days the clouds of sin and the problems of this world obscure our vision of Christ's light. Our Savior has promised to walk with us through every moment of every day and night on this earth. He sent the Holy Spirit to lead us and guide us through whatever troubles we face. We belong to Christ, and no sin, no darkness—not even death—can separate us from Him.

Dear Jesus,
on cloudy days,

dreary days,

and days when
I cannot feel Your presence,
shine Your light
upon my life
so I may bask
in the comfort
of Your love.
Amen.

Blessed by Giving

Acts 20:32–35

"It is more blessed to give than to receive" (Acts 20:35). St. Paul tells us that Jesus first spoke these words, so they must be true. As adults, we both have experienced the power of these words many times. As children, however, we weren't so sure we believed them. We both remember this Bible passage being held over our heads as a commandment rather than the promise it really is.

"Share with your siblings," our parents would tell us. "After all, it's more blessed to give than to receive." In our resentment over being forced to share our latest treasure, we would sometimes fail to experience the joy of giving.

A number of recent studies indicate that people who give money to charity and volunteer their time at church or in community service are less likely to become depressed than those who do not. The researchers who have conducted these studies are not writing from a religious perspective. They are making scientific observations that verify what Christians have been saying for years. It is a blessing to give and to share what we have with others. The act of giving blesses the giver as well as the one who receives.

Every one of us ought to experience the joy of giving. It doesn't matter how young or old we are, or how much or little we have to offer. Even the littlest children need to give. If you've ever received a handful of freshly picked dandelions or a homemade gift from your children, then you know the joy the act of giving brings to them.

As Christians, we have been blessed by God beyond measure. None of us can repay Jesus Christ for the sacrifice He has made on our behalf. We have received the promise of forgiveness and everlasting life. Nothing on this earth compares to these priceless treasures. When we ponder the wonder of what God has first done for us, a desire to share develops deep within us. Although our sin may sometimes cause us to feel guarded or greedy, when the love of Christ overwhelms us, we cannot help but want to share.

Acts 20:35 is not so much a commandment as it is a promise. It is a word of grace from the very mouth of our Savior. If you give, you will be blessed. You will be happier than if you hoard. You will experience the love of Christ on a deeper level than if you cautiously keep your gifts, talents, and money to yourself.

Whenever our son brings us another of his homemade gifts, we always try to respond with delight. He is learning the joy of giving and sharing from the abundance that God has first given him.

Thank You, Jesus,

for granting me the privilege of sharing
with others what You have first given me.
Amen.

Called

Matthew 4:18–22

Last summer, we were visiting with a friend in our neighborhood. As we chatted on the porch, our friend's four children raced around their spacious backyard playing a game of hide and seek. When dusk descended, our friend stepped to the edge of the porch, cupped her hands around her mouth, and bellowed, "Amy, Andy, Abby, Alice! Time to come in!"

We continued our conversation as sweaty children came trudging to the porch. "Hi, Amy. Hello, Abby. How are you, Alice?" we said. As the children made their way inside, our friend glanced around with a worried look on her face. "Hey, where's Andy?" she asked.

"Don't know," said Amy.

"He was hiding," said Abby.

"He's gonna be in trouble," said Alice.

"Andrew James, get in here this minute!" our friend shouted, with an obvious tone of concern in her voice.

Finally, a few minutes later, Andy sauntered across the yard. His mother glared at him with her arms folded across her chest. "Didn't you hear me calling? "

"Yes, Ma'am. I heard. But I was having so much fun," answered Andy.

"Why didn't you come? You had me worried to death."

"Well, umm," stammered Andy, obviously realizing that no excuse would be good enough for his mother.

Andy's tardy response to his mother reminds us of all those call passages in the Gospels. Jesus said, "Follow me." Peter, Andrew, James, John, and Matthew among others left jobs and family and immediately followed Jesus. No questions, no stall tactics, no apparent fears—just straight forward obedience.

Yet many of us respond to God's call the same way Andy responded to his mother. We hear God's call. We hear the invitation to follow, to dedicate our lives to loving Jesus and others—and we don't respond. We're too busy. We're having too much fun. We don't want to be bothered right now. We'll do it tomorrow.

Andy found his mother's call to come home bothersome. He probably did not realize that the reason she called him and became angry when he did not respond was because she loved him. As Christians, we are blessed to have a Savior who cares enough to call us. Jesus calls us to turn from the vain ambitions of this world and focus our hearts and minds on Him.

When Christians talk about being "called" by Christ, we often describe those tasks we perceive God is asking us to take on. In fact, being called is more about what our Savior wants to do for us than about what He wants us to do for Him (although that's important too). When Christ calls us, He gives of Himself. He calls us to come bask in His presence at worship. He calls us to eat, to gather with other believers and be nourished at His Holy Table. Christ calls us because He loves us and wants to keep us safe from all the dangers of this world.

Thank You, Jesus,

for loving me so much
that You call me to come to You.
Please, Jesus, when I don't respond to You
immediately,
keep calling!
Amen.

Clothed in Christ

Luke 12:27–28

We live in Wisconsin where cold weather is an inescapable reality. We both grew up in northern climates, and after 30 some years of enduring winter's chill, we find ourselves vowing every February that this will finally be the year we move to California.

Winters are even more difficult since we have become parents. Not only do we need to bundle up ourselves every time we step outside, we also need to make sure our son is properly clothed. Unfortunately, Sam has an aversion to boots and mittens. Even a simple trip to the grocery store becomes a torturous ordeal. "No boots," Sam declares. He seems perfectly content to step out into frigid temperatures barefoot.

We have noticed that many teenagers also prefer a minimal amount of outdoor winter clothing. Apparently big fuzzy boots and soft woolly hats are not "cool." It is better to endure a bit of frostbite than to suffer the taunts of one's ill-clad peers. As parents, we have grown beyond worrying about which winter clothes are in style. We just want to stay warm. Imagining what Sam will be like as a teenager sends a shiver down our spines.

The Bible uses the image of clothing to remind us of God's love and protection. St. Paul writes: "for all of you who were baptized into Christ have clothed yourselves with Christ" (Galatians 3:27). Those are comforting words! What can be warmer than the love of our Savior?

We live in a cold, bitter world. Sin swirls about us and numbs our senses. Although many times we would prefer to stay inside and shelter ourselves from the chill of this world, we know that God calls us to go out and share Christ's love with others. Because we are clothed with Christ, we have both protection and warmth to shield us from the bitter chill of sin.

Sometimes, however, we head out into the world dressed like teenagers. We shed the clothes God has given us to wear. When we encounter others in this world, they are unable to tell from our words and demeanor that we belong to Christ.

What's wonderful about the clothes God has given is that they don't wear out and they can't be lost. We may sometimes forget to put them on, but whenever the Holy Spirit calls us back home to God, chilled by our own stupidity, Christ stands ready to greet us like a parent at the door. He embraces us with His Word, He wraps His arms around us, and warms us with His love. Then He sends us back out into the world, clothed with the promises He gave us at our Baptism. He sends us out and asks that we share our clothes with others.

Thank You, merciful Savior,
> for wrapping me in Your Word
> > and
> warming me with the comfort of Your promises.
> Let me never forget that I am clothed in Christ.
> > Amen.

Judge Not

Matthew 7:1–5; Romans 3:21–26

We sometimes stop at the grocery store after we pick up our son from preschool. It's not the ideal time to shop—Sam is usually cranky and the store is often crowded. On one Friday afternoon, we stopped to buy a few essentials for dinner. Sam seemed unusually upset that day. He sat in the cart sobbing. We asked him what was wrong, but Sam refused to reply.

Meanwhile, passersby stared at us. We tried not to imagine what they were thinking. As we cruised through the dairy department, Sam screaming and sobbing, an older woman said to a friend, "I certainly wouldn't let my child act like that in public!" The second woman replied, "That little boy needs some discipline!"

That wasn't the first time we'd been judged based on our child's behavior. It's happened at the mall, family gatherings, and even at church. Each time, we take a deep breath and ask God to guide our words. We find it difficult to ignore the judgments of others, although we know it's the best tactic. Often, we feel hurt. Even worse, sometimes the judging words of others affect how we see our son.

Before we became parents, we tended to judge other parents as well. We'd look at screaming toddlers and vow that our future children would be better behaved. When Sam was an infant, easily contained in our arms, we had moments of shaking our heads at children who ran up and down the aisles at church.

Now that we've been parents for a while, we don't judge other parents. We know how hard parenting is. We know that often a child's behavior results from circumstances beyond a parent's control. That day in the grocery store, when Sam was crying uncontrollably, he was sick. We didn't know it at the time. No wonder he behaved badly. There's also another reason for not judging other people—Jesus said so.

In His sermon on the mount, Jesus said, "Do not judge, or you too will be judged. For the same way you judge others, you will be judged, and with the measure you use, it will be measured to you. Why do you look at the speck of sawdust in your brother's eye and pay no attention to the plank in your own eye? How can you say to your brother, 'Let me take the speck out of your eye,' when all the time there is a plank in your own eye? You hypocrite, first take the plank out of your own eye, and then you will see clearly to remove the speck from your brother's eye" (Matthew 7:1–5).

Jesus' command reminds us of two truths. First, we will be judged by the same rules with which we judge others. Imagine that for a moment. It's a frightening thought. Second, when we judge other people's "sinfulness," we are ignoring our own sins. When we make judgments about the way other parents raise their children, we often avoid looking at ourselves and how we relate to our own children.

The most persuasive reason for not judging others comes from the witness of Jesus' life, death, and resurrection. Because of what God did for us through Christ, we have been judged to be right before God. Despite our sinfulness, despite our unworthy nature, God forgives us and promises us life everlasting. Do we deserve it? No. Did we earn it? No. Is it ours? Yes. "This righteousness from God comes through faith in Jesus Christ to all who believe. There is no difference, for all have sinned and fall short of the glory of God, and are justified freely by His grace through the redemption that came by Christ Jesus" (Romans 3:22–24).

Dear Jesus,

when I am tempted to judge others,
let me remember Your grace toward me.
When I am being judged by others,
guide me to act with that same grace.
Amen.

Get Over It!

Ephesians 4:26–27; Matthew 18:15–18

Sometimes we get angry with our children because we love them so much. We invest our time and energy into providing and caring for them. We try to teach them to be responsible. We lecture, we joke, we gently prod. We do what we can to encourage their growth. Then they do or say something that reveals their immaturity. They shout at us, they break our favorite vase, they neglect to do their household chores. Their hurtful behavior may or may not be intentional. Our reaction is often automatic. Our body grows tense. Our heart beats faster. We may choke back tears or clench our fists. A flood of angry thoughts rolls through our mind.

God acknowledges anger as a fact of life. God also gives some practical solutions for dealing with it. St. Paul wrote, " 'In your anger do not sin': Do not let the sun go down while you are still angry, and do not give the devil a foothold" (Ephesians 4:26–27). In other words, get over it. Don't hang onto it. Don't go to bed angry.

We all know people who cling to their anger. They just can't let go of the fact that someone has hurt them. They hold onto their anger so intensely that it grows like a cancer which consumes them, leaving them bitter and unpleasant to be around.

Anger is an inevitable part of every family's life. When we love one another, we become vulnerable to getting hurt. Hurt leads to anger. And anger needs to be dealt with and diffused. The only way any relationship can thrive is when both parties are willing to acknowledge the anger, talk about it openly and compassionately, and then move beyond it.

In Matthew 18, Jesus instructs His followers to go to the one who has sinned against them. First, speak only to that one. If that doesn't work, bring one or two others along. If the person refuses to listen, tell it to the church. If it still doesn't work, "treat him as you would a pagan or a tax collector" (Matthew 18:17). This may be the first recorded example of "tough love." Hopefully, though, our family fights won't get this far. When we conscientiously work to discuss angry feelings with our children (and spouses), working toward common ground, we will often defuse the explosive anger and be able to move on to healthier relating.

In the midst of this—of being angry and working it out—it is helpful to remember the example of Jesus. When Jesus was dying on the cross, surrounded by the angry shouts of the crowd, He behaved in a most amazing way. Jesus said, "Father, forgive them for they do not know what they are doing" (Luke 23:34). No doubt our sinful behavior angers God again and again. But because of Christ's intercession, God does not stay angry with us. God forgives us and allows us to start anew.

We all might do well to post Paul's words in a prominent place in our homes: "'In your anger do not sin': Do not let the sun go down while you are still angry, and do not give the devil a foothold." With God's grace and the guidance of the Holy Spirit, these words can become a reality in the everyday life of the Christian family.

Dear Jesus,

help me to express my feelings of anger
the same way You did on the cross—
with compassion and a forgiving spirit.
Amen.

Watch Your Language!

Ephesians 4:29

A comic strip featured a man being yelled at by his boss. In the next frames, the man criticized his wife who screamed at their children who chased the dog who growled at the family cat who pursued a mouse. You may be thinking, "That's not a cartoon. That's my life!"

Most of us are trying to cope with myriad tasks and relationships. We juggle jobs, household chores, and our families. When life doesn't flow smoothly, our tempers may become short and our tongues become sharp. Our spouses and children often bear the brunt of our frustration. In time, taking out our frustrations on the ones we love can become our habitual way of coping with stress. Being critical of others becomes a habit like swearing or speeding. We fail to think before we speak. But it doesn't have to be this way. With the help of the Holy Spirit, bad habits can change into good ones.

St. Paul's words present us with a different way of behaving: "Do not let any unwholesome talk come out of your mouths, but only what is helpful for building others up according to their needs, that it may benefit those who listen" (Ephesians 4:29). Instead of hurling insults that pierce like arrows, comfort and encourage others with kind words that soothe like balm on a burning wound. Look at the needs of others and say only what is helpful for building up. Let your words convey grace like the grace God gives to you.

The next time you find yourself wanting to speak critical words to your spouse or children, stop and ask yourself, "Will these words build up? Do they convey Christ's love?" If the answer is "no," then ask Christ to help you speak kinder, gentler words. Pray that Jesus will guard and guide your speech.

Despite the best intentions, we all occasionally fail to follow Paul's admonition. Our sinful nature gets the best of us, and we speak before we think. In those moments, we need to ask both God and our family for forgiveness. In the act of seeking forgiveness from our spouse and children, God can bring good out of a difficult situation. When we seek forgiveness, God can open doors to greater communication and a deeper mutual understanding. God can lead us into new ways of relating to one another. And perhaps through the difficulty, we will grow in love, respect, and concern for our family members.

A final note about sin and forgiveness: in no way does God's forgiveness permit us to continue hurting one another. As Paul wrote, "What shall we say, then? Shall we go on sinning so that grace may increase? By no means! We died to sin; how can we live in it any longer?" (Romans 6:1–2).

The Greek word for "repent" means literally "to turn around" or change directions. When we repent and ask God and others for forgiveness, we are saying that through Him we want to turn our actions around. We want to speak kind words instead of cruel ones, give praise instead of criticism. Forgiveness wipes our slates clean with God. Asking for the forgiveness of others may give us a second chance with them as well. We will need God's help and guidance to do it, but with God's help all things are possible.

Jesus, teacher and friend,
guard and guide my speech
so what I say
will bring Your grace
to those who hear it.
Amen.

"Mr. Fix-It"

Sam came running with tears rolling down his cheeks. He held up his favorite book and pointed to a page that had been torn in two.

"I broke it," Sam wailed.

"It's okay," replied Rochelle. "Daddy can fix it with tape."

Sure enough, Harold found a roll of invisible tape and in a matter of seconds repaired Sam's "broken" book. Though Harold is not the world's most mechanically inclined father, Sam was impressed. "Daddy can fix things with tape," Sam proclaimed.

One day we packed Sam into our car for a trip to the grocery store. When we started the car, a loud roar came from the exhaust pipe. Harold stepped out of the car and noticed that the muffler was lying in the driveway. As we headed to the auto repair shop, Sam asked, "Why is the car growling?"

"It's broken," Rochelle replied.

"Daddy can fix it with tape," said Sam, ever confident in his father's abilities.

If only all household repairs were that simple. Unfortunately, many objects in our house have been broken and few of them can be fixed with tape.

The Bible tells us that material objects aren't the only things that get broken in this world. In fact, since Adam and Eve first disobeyed God, the whole human race has been broken. Every person who's ever lived on this earth (except One) has suffered from a broken relationship with God, other humans, and all creation. Since sin first entered our world, we humans are like pages that have been torn in two. Unlike those torn pages, however, our broken lives cannot be easily repaired. The rift runs deep.

The repair of our human brokenness is a job only God can do. When we humans try to "fix ourselves" without the help of our Savior, we might as well be trying to attach our mufflers to our cars with tape. Human solutions just don't hold.

That's why God sent our Savior Jesus Christ to come into this world to suffer and die for our sins. St. Paul describes Jesus' saving work on the cross as the act of "reconciliation" (see Romans 5:10–11 and 2 Corinthians 5:18–19). To reconcile means "to bring together." God sent Jesus to restore both our relationship with our heavenly Father and our relationships with one another.

God mends the torn pages of our lives, but it's not tape that holds us together—it's the very blood of Jesus. It doesn't matter how broken we may be, there's no damage Jesus can't repair.

Blessed Jesus, I am broken.

Mend me.

Heal me.

Make me whole.

Amen.

(Repeat this prayer throughout the day.)

Every Two Seconds

Psalm 139:13–16

Approximately every two seconds somewhere in the world, a baby is born. That's one second and two ... one second and two. Every two seconds another new life bursts forth, and a tiny set of lungs breathes in and out for the first time in this world. In the next hour another 1800 infants will have been born.

Some of these infants will be greeted with a mother's shout of joy, and others with sighs of disappointment. Some will be born into a life of prosperity, but many more will be born into poor families. Some babies will be held by a loving father, and others will never know if their father is even alive. Some will be fair-skinned; more will be dark. And all will be beautiful in God's eyes.

Unless you know a woman who is on the verge of giving birth, you will probably never know any of the infants being born as you read this devotion. Yet each one of them is known to God. And each one of them will always be loved by God, even if they are never loved by anyone else in this world.

One second and two ... it can be overwhelming when you think about it. So many new lives constantly coming into the world. How can God keep track of it all? Yet He does. God is present at the birth of each child, whether the delivery is taking place in a modern hospital room or in a shack with no running water.

Every birth, no matter what the circumstances, is a holy moment, because God is the Creator of all life. God is our heavenly Father, who loves all children, even the ones whose earthly fathers abandon them. Yet God also intimately understands the experience of being a mother bringing new life into this world. The Bible reminds us that ultimately God is the one who gives us birth (Deuteronomy 32:18) and comforts us "as a mother comforts her child" (Isaiah 66:13).

More important, God knows what it is like to be born into this world. In the life of our Savior Jesus Christ, God became "one with us." God became an infant and experienced fully both the joys and trauma of entering this life. This means that at the moment of birth, God understands completely the experiences of father, mother, and child.

Even more mind boggling is the fact that God knows each child even before he or she comes into this world (see Psalm 139). God knows everything about us. Of course, God's knowledge and care for us does not end at birth. Because Jesus lived, died, and rose again, we can be certain that He walks with us every step of our way through life, death, and beyond.

Prayer idea:

Take a few minutes and count to two
over and over,
remembering that each time you do,
another infant is entering the world.
Ask God to bless each of these children.

Bats in My Bed

Psalm 91

Our son had been having nightmares every night for almost a month. Because his favorite picture book told a story about bats, these frightening creatures flew into his dreams. Each night he would cry out, and we would walk into his room to find him standing beside his bed. "Can you get the bats out of my bed?" he would ask.

Sam was not fully awake and not sleeping either. In his mind (and in the dark), the little pink and blue teddy bears on his sheets looked like bats. We discovered that reasoning with Sam when he was in this "dream-waking" state was impossible. So we would sweep the "bats" off the bed and shoo them out the window. We'd tuck Sam back into bed and kiss him good night. We'd say a prayer with him, asking God to keep the bats busy outside the house.

Sam is not the first child to have bad dreams. Almost every parent (and baby sitter) has experienced the fear in a child having a night terror. Even adults have horrible dreams. One night Rochelle dreamed Sam had been stolen from us in the middle of a busy hotel. She screamed and begged for him to appear, but he was lost. When Rochelle woke, her heart was jumping and her mind racing. She crept down the hall to make sure Sam was sleeping safely in his bed. He was. But she was not calmed. She lay awake until dawn, held captive by the chill of that dream.

The psalmist must have known this fear when writing Psalm 91. This psalm reminds us of God's protection: God "will cover you with His feathers, and under His wings you will find refuge; His faithfulness will be your shield and rampart. You will not fear the terror of night, nor the arrow that flies by day" (Psalm 91:4–5).

A friend of ours has carried a typed copy of this psalm, a gift from her grandmother, in her wallet for more than 20 years. She says it reminds her Who's in charge of her life. These words from the Bible help her recall that she really has no reason to feel afraid or anxious—for God will protect her.

Many of us experience fear in the form of nightmares. Many more of us experience anxiety in facing day to day life. We are stressed by the large number of choices we must make each day. Holiday seasons and other special occasions can multiply the anxiety we feel. We may experience such a great amount of stress that we don't enjoy the preparation (let alone the holiday).

This psalm can reassure us in the midst of nightmares and daytime fear and anxiety. It reminds us that we are never alone. Although God does not always remove our nightmares or anxieties, God does help us to cope with them, overcome them, and sometimes even learn from them. Each day and each night, we rest in the shadow of the One who will always watch over us and provide for us—the Almighty.

The Bible says "perfect love drives out fear" (1 John 4:18). None of us loves perfectly, but we are all perfectly loved. We are loved by a perfect Savior and by a gracious and all-powerful God. Listen: "I will say of the LORD, 'He is my refuge and my fortress, my God, in whom I trust'" (Psalm 91:2).

Protecting God,
guard me and my family
day and night
so we are not afraid.
In Jesus' name. Amen.

Come, Lord Jesus

Matthew 18:19–20

On Tuesday at 5:48 P.M. the Johnson family gathered at the supper table after a long day of work, study, and play. Todd, age 37, and Jan, 36, both endured grueling days at their respective places of employment. Thirteen-year-old Mary spent the day at school, followed by a long workout at basketball practice. Her brother John also attended school and will be heading off for his piano lesson in 30 minutes. Kyle, the youngest, had a difficult day at preschool, suffering an embarrassing accident just when he thought he had mastered that dreaded potty.

Before digging into their hastily prepared dinner of macaroni and cheese, green beans, and milk, the Johnson family quickly spoke together the words of a prayer they recite every night: "Come Lord Jesus, be our guest, and let these gifts to us be blessed. Amen." As they prayed, not one of the Johnsons paid close attention to the words they were speaking. Still, Someone wanted them to know that He heard their every word.

"Yes Kyle, most certainly. I accept your invitation. I enjoy being a guest at your supper table. I love watching you and your family talk and laugh together. But I notice that tonight you're not your usual bubbly self. Kyle, my child, I know your hopes and I know your fears. I promise you need not be afraid of that 'monster' beneath your bed. My love is stronger than the troubles that bother you. Don't worry about that 'accident' either. It will all come together in time.

"John, my child, I accept your invitation. I enjoy watching you grow, as you develop that talent I've given you. I know your hopes and I know your fears. Keep at your piano lessons, John. I can see that sometimes you don't feel like practicing. I know you hate it when others tease you about your piano playing. I understand what it feels like to be laughed at. Don't quit! I will give you the perseverance to go on.

"Dear Mary, yes, I accept your invitation. I will bless the food on your plate. You certainly need to eat well after that difficult workout. Mary, my child, I know your hopes and I know your fears. I assure you that you need not be so concerned about what your friends think of you. I know you believe God made your feet too large and your nose too long. I wish you could see yourself the way I see you. So beautiful and so graceful out there on the basketball court.

"Todd and Jan, of course, I accept your invitation. I know tonight it was Todd's turn to cook and the macaroni's not quite done. Don't be upset, I will bless this meal you eat. Filet mignon or beans and rice—I'm not picky. I will come and feast with all who invite me. Lately I have seen how the two of you are fretting. I know the bills are due and your money is in short supply. I take care of the tiniest birds and flowers. I will surely provide for you.

"Todd and Jan, my children, look at each other. Look around this table. See how I've blessed you. I know you both sometimes worry that the love has gone out of your marriage. I will see you through the difficult times. Remember when Mary got sick? I was with you then, and I am with you now. I will be, I promise, forever.

"Thank you, my children. Thank you for the invitation. I know your hopes and I know your fears, and I love you just the same. Even as you invite Me, I invite you to the Holy Meal of My body and blood."

Prayer idea:

Say one of your favorite table graces,

right now.

"Come and See"

John 1:43–51

When Harold's sister arrived from California for a visit, our son took great delight in showing his aunt around our house. Together the two of them watched Sam's favorite videos and read Sam's favorite books. They nibbled on some of Sam's favorite snacks and played many of Sam's favorite games. We think Sam's aunt enjoyed herself, though she did look a bit weary after reading *Frog and Toad Are Friends* for the tenth consecutive time. We certainly enjoyed the visit. A week of free baby-sitting meant we finally had time to attend to some long neglected tasks.

As we watched Sam interact with his aunt, we noted that he truly enjoyed sharing with her those things he treasures most in his life. "Come and see this book," he shouted as he bounced up and down, unable to contain his excitement.

Sam is not so different from the rest of us. Most of us, whatever our age, enjoying showing off those things we most value. "Come and see my new car," we tell our friends. For what fun is a new car if there's no one to show it to? If we buy a new home, we throw a house-warming party and proudly display our new abode to our closest friends and family members. Many of us parents delight in pulling out our wallets and showing off the latest photos of our children. Indeed, what fun is anything if we keep it locked up, and allow no one else to see it? There's something in our very human nature which makes us want to show others those things we value most.

The gospel writer John tells about someone who shared a recently discovered treasure. A man named Philip was so excited that he found his friend Nathanael and said, "Come and see" (John 1:46). What Philip wanted Nathanael to see was actually a person, a man named Jesus, whom Philip knew to be the Messiah, the promised Savior. As he brought skeptical Nathanael to meet Jesus, Philip became one of the first evangelists—sharing his enthusiasm for Jesus with others.

We have a friend who keeps a picture of Jesus in her wallet. When she shows off her photos of her loved ones, she includes the picture of Jesus and says, "He's one of my family members too." This way she shows others that Jesus is the One she values most of all.

What parts of your life do you most often invite others to come and see? Do you share your faith in Jesus as your Savior or do you keep it to yourself? Do you tell others about Jesus the way you'd tell them about your new car or other prized possessions? While you don't need to work Jesus' name into every conversation, life presents us all with many opportunities to share the love of the One who gave His life for us, the One who invites everyone to "come and see" all He has done for us.

> **Jesus,** You are the greatest treasure of my life.
> Grant me the enthusiasm
> to share You and Your love with others.
> Amen.

Back to the Basics

Psalm 65:5–13

We once overheard a conversation between two children which made us chuckle but also made us wonder.

"Where does bacon come from?" asked one.

"Don't you know?" replied the other. "Bacon comes from the meat department."

"What about eggs? Do they come from the meat department?"

"No," said the other. "Those are in the dairy aisle."

We chuckled because we both grew up in rural areas but now live in the city. We can hardly imagine two children having this same discussion on the farm. This conversation also reminded us that many of us (not just those who live in urban areas) have lost touch with the origin of life's basic necessities.

One hundred years ago, if people needed a new table for their dining room, they may very well have built it themselves. Today, if we need a new table, many of us just stop by the nearest furniture store and purchase it already made. One hundred years ago, when much of our nation was still rural, many people would collect their eggs each day from the hens on their farm. Today most of us buy our eggs at the supermarket.

Times have changed. We are not suggesting that we abandon modern conveniences. Yet in this era of microwave ovens and personal computers, we can easily forget the origin of all our blessings. For example, someone might ask, "How did you get your new television?" We might reply, "I bought it with money I earned from working." We might feel the television belongs to us since we worked for our money and deserve it.

Yet as Christians, we cannot say that anything we own truly belongs to us. God gives us the ability to work and use the money we earn to purchase what we own. As Christians, we know that God, and God alone, is the origin of all our blessings. All we have and are, even our very lives, has been given to us—loaned to us—by our gracious Maker and Provider.

Sometimes, we live as though our money, our possessions, and our time belong solely to us. We all face the temptation to use these gifts selfishly, for our own pleasure, without regard for God or others. In our modern world, it's too easy to gulp down our double cheeseburgers without even a silent word of thanks to God for providing our daily bread. It's too easy to race around the mall, spending our money as though we have an endless supply of it. It's too easy to stare at the television for hours, and end up wondering why we have no time to pray and read the Bible.

When we do read the Bible (especially the book of Psalms), God helps us rediscover that He is the One who provides us with all good things. Do your children know where bacon comes from? (We're not talking about pigs.) Do they know where the miracles of modern medicine and the advances of modern technology originate? (It's not in the mind of a scientist.) Do they know Who orders and numbers each day? (It's not a time management consultant.)

Let's get back to the basics and thank the One who puts bread on all our tables (yes, even the tables we buy at the store) and nourishes us with the Bread of life.

Thank You, Lord, for daily bread,
—for work and play,
food and shelter,
family and friends.

Thank You, Lord, for everything! In Jesus' name. Amen.

Nothing Shall Separate Us

Romans 8:35–39

Our son was at that age. At least that's what we kept telling ourselves. And others. "He's 3," we would tell people. "You know 3." And they would nod their heads compassionately. One friend even said, "You have my sympathy."

One Sunday morning when Sam was "at that age," Rochelle rose from the pew at the appropriate time to head to the altar for Holy Communion. She held out her hand for Sam, expecting him to follow.

"NO!" he shouted.

"Sam, it's time for you to receive a blessing," explained Rochelle.

"Noooooooo! I don't want a blessing. I want to stay here," shouted Sam.

People waited behind him. Sam was holding up the line. Finally, after begging and pleading, Rochelle left him in the pew and headed toward the altar alone. As she walked up the aisle, her gaze kept drifting backward. Would he be okay? Would he be afraid? Rochelle hadn't realized how tall the pews were and how short Sam was until she left him alone in the pew and started walking. He disappeared from sight.

As Rochelle knelt to receive Communion, she glanced over her shoulder to check on Sam. She knelt and prayed, keeping one eye on God and one eye on Sam. Another parishioner who saw her worry, put her arm around Rochelle and said, "He's doing fine."

When Rochelle returned to the pew, Sam was peering around anxiously, looking for his mommy. But he was okay. He wasn't hurt or afraid.

Sam was at that age. You know, that age where children are more interested in their own wants and needs than anything else. As adults, we haven't completely lost that self-centeredness—we still yearn to do our own things. More often, we are divided. Our attention is split between many competing interests: children, home, work, and God.

Many parents have experienced those moments of being at the communion rail but having only one eye on God. The other eye, the other part of our vision and attention, is somewhere else. Perhaps we're thinking about Sunday dinner, worrying about our job, or, like Rochelle, concerned about our children. Whatever the cause, our interest is divided ... and we may feel separated from God.

In Romans 8, St. Paul reminds us that many things may try to separate us from God's love in Christ Jesus. Many things may *try*. But they cannot win. God is always stronger. We may feel our attention is divided—but God's is not. Through Jesus Christ, God continues to love and care for us even when we might feel cut off from Him. In those moments when sins, worries, or the concerns of this world seek to get between us and Jesus, we can be certain our Savior always has both eyes on us. Jesus gives us His complete attention, even when He doesn't have ours.

Thank You, God,

for Your promise
that nothing
shall separate me
from Your love in Christ Jesus—
neither
(name problems that sometimes trouble you) ...
nor ... nor ...
In Jesus' name I pray.
Amen!

Why?

Matthew 2:13–18; Romans 8:35–39

We sit at the breakfast table reading the morning paper. We see news of a killing, a senseless drive-by murder in a neighborhood not too far from our own. An 8-year-old child struck down by an errant bullet. We see a photo of a sobbing mother above a one-word headline: "WHY?"

We see these images every day. In our violent, sensationalized culture, we easily become desensitized to the evil that surrounds us. Then, every so often, one of the stories hits close to our heart. A child is murdered just miles from where we live. And we realize that none of us is immune to the pain.

Modern day prophets proclaim that the world is becoming a violent place. But it's always been this way. We hardly need to turn to our newspapers to read about acts of violence. Some of humanity's most dastardly deeds are recorded right in the Bible. The Bible tells it as it was—and still is. The same book which comforts us in times of trouble and recounts God's incredible acts of mercy reminds us that the world in which we live has fallen far short of God's intentions.

One of the most troubling Biblical stories for parents is the account of the "slaughter of the innocents" recorded in Matthew 2:13–18. When King Herod learned Jesus had been born, he ordered that all boys, ages 2 and under, be murdered. Jesus escaped to Egypt with Mary and Joseph, while many other Jewish children met senseless, violent deaths.

Any caring parent can feel the utter grief recorded in Matthew 2:18: "Rachel weeping for her children and refusing to be comforted, because they are no more." If there had been newspapers in those days, they would have asked the same question that plagues us today: Why? Why would God allow His Son to escape while those poor little babies died?

While we cannot completely understand the mystery of God's ways, the answer to this question is found throughout the New Testament. Jesus escaped Herod's bloody decree because His time had not yet come to suffer. And He did suffer. On Calvary's cross, Jesus became the ultimate victim of senseless violence. Yet in the end, God made sense of the senselessness. Three days later, Christ rose to life again and thereby conquered the power of sin and death.

Senseless violence continues to plague our world. The question stills rings out: WHY? Rachel still weeps for her children. In our pain, we trust that one day the senselessness will make sense to us just as it does to God. As we look forward to that day when Christ will come again to abolish all suffering, we know that in the meantime "neither death nor life ... will be able to separate us from the love of God that is in Christ Jesus our Lord" (Romans 8:38–39).

Dear God,

as a parent,
my heart aches
for those who have lost children.

Please comfort all who mourn
the loss of their young ones,
and give them the peace
only You can provide
through Jesus Christ our Lord.
Amen.

Leaves!

Isaiah 40:6–8

We are blessed with three large, lovely trees around our house. These trees represent a lifetime of growing. They provide abundant shade for us and our neighbors in the summer. In the winter, we gaze up at them, marvel at their strength, and applaud the beauty of their branches. The only time we have ever felt anything but deep appreciation for these trees is in the autumn, when their leaves come fluttering down and cover our lawn like thick carpeting.

Every autumn it's the same story. Each of the three trees turns color and loses its leaves in succession. For more than two months we rake leaves. Or we would rake leaves—if we could. Truth is, Rochelle is allergic to almost every blooming thing. And both of us suffer from allergies to the wet, moldy leaves. So we hire teenagers to rake.

Despite our best efforts, we are always a bit behind on our leaves. In our city, we rake the leaves out to the street. Then a city vehicle comes by to gather them up and turn them to mulch. Each year, our leaves sit for a time before they are raked to the street. Then the wind comes and swirls them into our neighbors' yards. So our poor neighbors, who enjoy our trees' shade in the summer, also reap the bounty of our leaves in the fall. Sometimes they complain good-naturedly about our sharing our leaves with them. Mostly they just rake them up.

Each autumn we watch the leaves turn and fall. We see our flowers fade, wither, and die. We notice that our grass has turned brown. We sit and gaze at the wind, carrying away the beautiful piles of leaves we have made in front of the house. We know that all things on earth cycle through life and death, and yet it is hard to take. We feel a bit of a pang when summer waves its last good-bye. We grieve the shortening of the days.

We worry about our own lives and deaths. Will we stay healthy? For how long? Will we live to see our children grown? Not one of us knows the answers to these questions. We do know that none of us will live on this earth forever.

We find comfort in God's promise: "The grass withers, the flower fades; but the Word of our God will stand forever" (Isaiah 40:8 NRSV). Things on this earth will not live forever. We are constantly reminded of this basic truth, not just in autumn. Toys break. Cars rust. Dust settles all around. But God's Word, God's promises, will never die. God lives within us and walks beside us as we pass through the seasons of life. And because of Jesus, because of His death and resurrection, we are assured of everlasting life. For we who trust in Jesus Christ, death is not the end.

Each spring, when buds burst forth on our trees, we celebrate the new life that only God can give. We know those tender buds will one day become rotting leaves tossed by the wind to our neighbors' yards. But because of Christ, we will not meet a similar fate. Death will not be the end of us. Christ is risen. He is risen indeed. And we too shall rise. Alleluia!

Dear Jesus,

when all around me seems to be dying,
remind me that through Your death
and resurrection I have new life in You.
Amen.

Waiting
—An Advent Celebration

Psalm 62

On the first day of November, we headed to the mall to purchase a wedding gift for a friend. Just days before, we had shopped at the same mall for a birthday gift. It had been decorated with signs of autumn and Halloween, pumpkins, and Indian corn. That night, we opened the door and were bombarded by loud Christmas music, flashing lights, and oversized candy canes hung from the ceiling. Each store featured special Christmas displays and holiday offers.

"Is today Christmas?" asked Sam.

"No, Honey, not yet," answered Rochelle.

"Tomorrow, then? Will we have Christmas tomorrow?"

It's no secret that our holiday seasons are run by commercial organizations determined to turn a profit. They want to create an urgency in the buyers. They want consumers to believe they are ever behind in their shopping schedule. Last year, this hit us right between the eyes. Since we were busy (and short on funds) during early December, we decided to wait until after Christmas Day to buy gifts for the relatives we were traveling to see after the holiday.

On December 26th we entered the mall, hoping to glimpse one last look at the poinsettias, waiting to hear the joyful Christmas songs. The mall had been stripped clean of decorations. The candy canes had been removed and in their place hung large red and silver foil hearts.

As Christian parents, we need to consider how we want to celebrate major holidays with our children. We have decided that each year we will observe the Advent season together. We hope these days before Christmas will be like a small island of rest, a quiet place from which we can prepare to celebrate the birth of our Savior.

We hope to teach our son about the power of waiting. We can tell him how the people of Israel wandered for 40 years, waiting to enter the Promised Land. We can remind him about the people waiting for the Messiah, longing for a Savior. We can wait together, praying and hoping for the Savior who comes into our hearts each Christmas (each day, really). We can teach our son that as Christians, we await that day when Jesus will come again to create a new heaven and a new earth. And we can rejoice as a family, "My soul finds rest in God alone; my salvation comes from Him" (Psalm 62:1).

You can do something to celebrate Advent this year. Light candles on an Advent wreath each week. Open doors on an Advent calendar each day. Borrow books from your church or library about the season. Have an Advent festival in your home, reading, singing, and praying together. Take on a special task as a family, such as collecting money or making a gift for a family in need.

Whatever you do, see what happens when you wait until December 25th to celebrate Christmas. Then, when the day finally arrives (it may seem like an eternity to your children), rejoice in your Savior's birth. Throw a party! Let it last 12 days. The decorations at the mall may be gone, but Jesus will be around forever.

God of our salvation,
    I wait with silent anticipation
    for the coming of Your Son. **Amen.**

Sweetly Sleeping Christmas Angel

2 Corinthians 4:6–12

On Christmas Eve, we headed off to church more than an hour before the service was to start. Almost-4-year-old Sam had to put on his Christmas angel costume for the Sunday school program. Sam had vowed for two weeks that he was not going to participate. We practiced singing at home every day. He knew the music by heart. However, he had refused to try on his costume at practice. In fact, he'd refused to even stand with the other children.

When we arrived at church, Rochelle asked Sam, "Do you want to see your teachers?"

"Yes!" shouted Sam.

We headed to the Sunday school rooms. As soon as Sam saw his best friend, Jacki, wearing her angel costume, he was hooked. "Put mine on, please!" he said.

On it went, over his head. Sam and Jacki danced around the room, sparkling and glittering, too busy to even stand still for a picture. Half an hour later, we watched from our seats in the sanctuary as Sam marched in with the rest of the Sunday school children. Fifteen minutes after that, just before the children were scheduled to sing, Sam's teacher tapped Rochelle on the shoulder. In her arms she held our slumbering angel. Almost-4-year-old Sam slept in Rochelle's arms until just before it was time for Holy Communion.

Throughout the service, holding Sam tightly in her arms, Rochelle was reminded of these words from Hebrews: "Are not all angels ministering spirits sent to serve those who will inherit salvation?" (Hebrews 1:14). Parenting an almost-4-year-old is not easy. Our days were fraught with difficult moments—timeouts and temper tantrums to spare. Rochelle believed that on Christmas she had been ministered to by an angel. Sam, dressed like the cherub he so often wasn't, slept sweetly in her arms—a privilege we had thought long gone. There is nothing so joyous, we think, as holding our sleeping child in our arms. Almost-4-year-olds are not usually up for much holding. God had provided for Rochelle and Sam this one sweet moment. Of course, it didn't last.

Sam woke up just before Communion and shouted for the whole congregation to hear, "Take it off! I'm done being an angel!"

Rochelle remembered enough of Sam's goodness and her love for him to patiently lead him out of church until he could calm down.

Sleeping angel and screaming demon. The reformer Martin Luther reminded his hearers that Christians are always caught in the paradox of being both saint and sinner. We are ultimately freed from the power of sin through Jesus' death and resurrection. We are also bound to sin through our fallen human condition.

We often see this paradox in our son's behavior and in our own. Sometimes we come close to being what God wants us to be. At other times, we fail miserably. Saint and sinner—we are never just one or the other.

In the heat of parenting, with our child shrieking, "I'm done being an angel," we might have trouble remembering that this little one is not only a sinner, but one of God's redeemed saints. Rochelle's moment with Sam, the sleeping angel, reminded her to look for the goodness in him—even when his behavior is far from perfect. It also reminded us that one day, through Christ, we will finally become everything God wants us to be. On that wonder-filled day, we will join with the angels and the saints, singing 'round our Savior's throne.

God of both saints and sinners, **open my eyes** to see the goodness in all Your children, through Jesus Christ my Lord. **Amen.**

"You Don't Understand"

On Christmas Eve, the 5-year-old son of one of our friends tossed in his bed with eyes wide open, impatiently praying for morning to come. When his mother came to check on him, he asked, "What time are we getting up in the morning? Three o'clock?"

"Oh no," mother laughed. "It will still be dark then."

"How about five o'clock?" he asked.

"No," his mother replied firmly. "We'll all get up at seven. You need to learn to be patient."

"But Mom," our friend's son pleaded, "You don't understand. It's hard to be a kid on Christmas Eve."

Just about every parent has heard the words, "you don't understand." Yet it's not just children who utter that phrase. At different times in various ways, all of us feel alone and misunderstood. Many times we have heard others tell us, "You just don't understand what it's like to be divorced ... or to be unemployed ... or to watch a loved one slowly die from cancer."

Truly none of us can completely understand another human's experience. Each one of us faces unique situations, and try as we may, none of us can walk completely in the shoes of another. Yet there is One who does understand.

The Bible says that because Jesus Himself suffered when He was tempted, He is able to help us in our moments of weakness (Hebrews 2:18). Jesus is described as "Immanuel" which means "God with us" (Matthew 1:23). Jesus came to earth to face every pain and every joy, every hope and every fear, which we experience as humans. Jesus understands us.

Jesus knows what it's like to be 5 years old, and unable to fall asleep at night. Jesus knows what it's like to be a teenager, totally misunderstood by his parents. Jesus knows what it is like to feel lonely and burdened. Jesus knows anger. Jesus knows joy. Jesus knows the empty silence and overwhelming sadness of death. Jesus knows temptation. Finally, Jesus knows pain, abandonment, and humiliation. He died like a criminal on a cross for all the world to see.

There exists no human feeling or emotion, no human experience of any kind, which Jesus does not understand. And because Jesus ultimately conquered our greatest enemy—eternal death—by his resounding resurrection, we need never feel alone again.

We know we are loved by a Savior who does understand. Christ walks with us, even through life's darkest moments. That's the miracle that sustains us whether we're 5, 95, or anywhere in between.

Jesus,

You know me better than I know myself.
You know me at my best
and You know me at my worst.
Thank You for loving me **always**
and for understanding all that I experience
in this life.
Amen.

The Gratitude Box

Colossians 1:3–9

A few years ago our family started the practice of giving one another a few homemade Christmas gifts. One of the gifts we make each year is a gratitude box. We wrap the top and bottom of a plain box so it can be opened by simply lifting the lid. On 12 index cards, we all write reasons why we are grateful for each of the other people in our family. Then we place these cards in the box.

On Christmas morning and on each day of Christmas until Epiphany, we open the box and read some of the cards. We do this to remind ourselves that our commitment to Christ includes loving and honoring one another (see 1 John 4:21). One of the ways we can demonstrate our love for others is by reminding both them and ourselves why we are thankful for their presence in our lives.

In Paul's letter to the Ephesians, he wrote, "I have not stopped giving thanks for you, remembering you in my prayers" (Ephesians 1:16). Paul and Timothy began their letter to the church at Colosse with similar words: "We always thank God, the Father of our Lord Jesus Christ, when we pray for you, because we have heard of your faith in Christ Jesus and of the love you have for all the saints" (Colossians 1:3–4). In fact, many of Paul's letters begin with a prayer of thanksgiving for the readers.

This "attitude of gratitude" can serve as a model for Christians (and especially Christian families) in our life together. Sometimes in the daily grind of family life, we lose sight of just how much we value our loved ones. We easily take the love and ongoing presence of our family for granted. Sometimes we may even be kinder to strangers than to our own families. We may scream at our loved ones for misplacing the remote control and grumble about their muddy footprints on the kitchen floor. Then we answer the telephone and talk to a stranger with a voice so sweet it sounds like we've been eating honey.

God has given us the gift of our families to enrich our lives. God wants us to treasure one another just as He treasures us. This year, we will again fill our gratitude box and place it under the Christmas tree beside the other gifts. We know families who participate in a similar, less formal practice. Around the supper table each night, they take time to talk about why they are grateful for one another. These sorts of rituals help us put family life in perspective—God's perspective.

Are you thankful for your family? Then tell them. Right now if you can. Tell God too. God also likes to know you appreciate all He has given you.

Thank You, God,

for the gift of my family.
I really do love them,
although I don't always tell them
or show them I do.

Today (and every day),
remind me to let each member of my family
know how thankful I am for his or her presence
in my life.

In Jesus' name.
Amen.

God's Big Hug

Luke 15:11–31

Our son sat on the timeout step, and shouted, "Mommy! Daddy! I'm sorry! Big hug! I'm sorry! Big hug!" He knew the ritual. When Sam does something inappropriate, he takes a timeout to reflect on his behavior. Then, either Mommy or Daddy talks to him about it. After a long talk and sometimes more quiet reflection, Sam says "I'm sorry" and receives a big hug. Sam's ritual when he misbehaves reminds us of our own relationship with our merciful and forgiving God.

In the parable of the prodigal son, Jesus describes a tangible image of God's forgiveness. In the story, the younger son wasted his resources. When he had lost all he had, he decided he must go home, confess his sins to his father, and beg his forgiveness. Before the son even reached the door, his father spotted him and "was filled with compassion for him; he ran to his son, threw his arms around him and kissed him" (Luke 15:20b).

The father then provided for his son tangible and generous signs of his forgiveness—the best robe, a ring, and sandals to wear, a fattened calf to eat, music, and dancing. Together they feasted. When the father saw the son returning home—a sign to his father that he had repented—he felt compassion for his son. He welcomed him with a big hug, an all-encompassing embrace. The father gave his forgiveness lavishly. He did not lecture the son or berate him. Instead, he rejoiced in his presence and gave him the best he had to offer.

In this story, we learn about God's attitude toward us when we turn away. We are all sinners. We all turn from God who is our home. Like the prodigal son, we wander lost and alone. We look for other things to take the place of God in our lives—material goods, sex, alcohol and drugs, money, and prestige.

When this happens, the Holy Spirit leads us to gaze about and see that we are far from home. With the Spirit's help, we *turn around* and face toward home. We repent of our sins. The Greek word for repent literally means "to turn or return." When the prodigal son *turned* toward home, he had already repented of his sins. When God sees us turn toward Him, God has compassion for us and lavishly forgives us.

Probably the most difficult lesson we have learned as parents is that we often fail the ones we love. Each day, we try to live as Christian parents, serving God by caring for our child. We do not always do well at this task. We do not love God with our whole heart and we do not love Sam as we ought. In those moments, we take time to return to God, repent of our sins, and ask God for forgiveness. In Sam's language, we say we are sorry and ask for a "big hug." And God who loves us, draws us close, forgives our sins, and in the name of our Savior welcomes us home again.

Heavenly Father,

> when I stray far from home,
> remind me of Your love
> > and forgiveness
> > > so I may not fear turning back
> > > > to You.

In Jesus' name. Amen.

Never Alone

John 16:17–33

We can't quite say how it happened. Thunder crashed, lightning flashed, and rain poured freely from the sky. Sam was sleeping soundly through it all, enjoying his afternoon nap.

Rochelle heard the screaming first. She found Sam standing alone in the hallway, shaking from head to foot, and sobbing. Rochelle picked up Sam, carried him to the sofa, and held him. He kept saying, "I was alone. I was scared. Mommy don't let go."

Thunderstorms can be scary. Actually, much of life can seem scary. Doctor visits, dental appointments, meetings with the boss, school conferences, or even driving somewhere by ourselves. At some point in our lives, we will hear the thunder, look around, and see that we are alone.

Jesus talked about this in John's gospel. He said to the disciples, "But a time is coming, and has come, when you will be scattered, each to his own home. You will leave Me all alone" (John 16:32a). That very night Jesus was betrayed, arrested, and abandoned by His disciples. But the verse doesn't end there. Jesus went on to say, "Yet I am not alone, for My Father is with Me" (John 16:32b).

Even when we feel abandoned by our friends and family, we are never truly alone. Jesus stands beside us. Our Savior knows what it feels like to face trouble, to look around and realize that He is standing all by Himself. He bore the weight of our human sinfulness alone as He died abandoned on the cross. Even in our loneliest moments, we've never been as alone as Jesus was on Calvary. His cry, "My God, My God, why have You forsaken Me?" (Matthew 27:45) was the loneliest cry ever uttered on this earth. Jesus knows true loneliness, and He promises never to abandon us. Our risen Savior's promise, "And surely I am with you always, to the very end of the age" (Matthew 28:20), is one we can all take to heart.

We can find comfort in knowing that Jesus is always present, granting us grace sufficient for the moment. We need not fear anything in this life or the next. We need not fear for our children. We may not always be able to come running when they call out for help, but Jesus will be there for them. As He is for us. Whether it's thunderstorms or the very shadow of death we're facing, Jesus holds us close, never letting us go.

Lord Jesus,
> though others may fail me and desert me,
> You will never abandon me.

Thank You, Jesus, for this promise.
Amen.

A Letter to Our Young Friend, Hannah (On Her Confirmation Day)

Luke 18:15–17

Hey there, Hannah—

We can hardly believe you're a teenager already. Why, we still remember you toddling around your house in diapers (okay, we won't get into that). You certainly have been growing up fast. It wasn't so long ago that you were baptized.

As you now know, on that day God promised to provide for you always, forgive your sins, deliver you from evil, and bring you to everlasting life. Now you are ready to embrace God's wonderful promises by making a few of your own—confirming the faith the Holy Spirit first gave you on that day when you were washed in Christ's living water.

A lot of people think that confirming one's faith is a mark of maturity, a sign of growing up. This is most certainly true. You have grown, Hannah—both in stature and in faith. Very soon you'll be driving a car and then heading off to college. But on this your Confirmation day, we'd like to remind you of something Jesus told His disciples: "I tell you the truth, anyone who will not receive the kingdom of God like a little child will never enter it" (Luke 18:17).

Jesus was talking about faith, about trusting in His promises, about the very faith which you will confess today. He makes no mention of maturity or adult-like behavior. He simply says that we who trust in Him must believe like children.

Jesus reminds us that Confirmation is not about becoming an adult. It is about never forgetting that you are already a child of God. It is a reminder to never lose that childlike faith you already possess—the faith God gave you on the day you were baptized.

Hannah—you will learn and grow much more in the years

to come. You are well on your way to becoming an adult. And you will pass through many stages in your life. There will be changes in the way you look and think and act. But you will always be a child of God.

Don't let our society's signs of adulthood fool you. Don't let getting your driver's license, or voting for the first time, or graduating from high school fool you. Don't let the day you start your first job, or move into your own home, or hold your very own newborn child in your arms fool you. Long after you discover your first gray hair (arghh!), and long after you reach middle age, even long after you retire, you, like the rest of us, will always be God's child.

So when you stand before the congregation and confess your faith in Jesus Christ this morning, you don't need to act mature or adult-like. Just be yourself. Share with us the faith you already possess. And as you do, God will work through you to teach those of us who think we are adults, who think we're so mature and grown-up what the faith of a child is all about.

Love, your friends, Rochelle and Harold

Heavenly Father,

as I watch my children grow
(and as I see myself grow older too)
I thank You for promising that no matter how
many years go by, I will always be
Your very own baptized and redeemed child,
through Jesus Christ my Lord.
Amen.

Waiting by the Window

Matthew 24:42–44

"Emily's coming! Emily's coming!"

Our son could barely contain his excitement. At breakfast, we told him his favorite playmate, Emily, and her mother would be arriving at our house for a visit. As soon as he heard this, Sam ran to his favorite perch by the picture window at the front of our house. Every time he saw a car pass on the street outside, Sam shouted, "It's Emily!" Unfortunately, Emily wasn't scheduled to arrive for another hour, which can seem almost as long as eternity when you are 3 years old.

"Why don't you do something else until they come?" we suggested. Sam could focus on nothing but Emily's arrival. For 10 minutes, then 30, and finally 45, Sam watched and waited. With agonizing anticipation, his eyes remained fixed on the street outside.

As we observed our son watching for his friend, we remembered Jesus' words, "Therefore keep watch, for you do not know on what day your Lord will come" (Matthew 24:42). As Christians, we believe and confess that our resurrected Lord will return to this earth one day just as He promised.

Most of us do not sit by the window waiting for Jesus like Sam waited for Emily. Yet throughout history, many people have been obsessed with our Lord's return. Some have even attempted to predict the exact date of this event using the Scriptures. Many of these attempts have generated fear and anxiety about situations that are beyond our human control.

A popular rumor states that Martin Luther was once asked what he would do if he knew Jesus were returning tomorrow. He replied that he would plant a tree. Luther's remark gets at the heart of what Jesus meant when He told us to "keep watch." Because only our heavenly Father knows what the future will bring (Matthew 24:36), it doesn't help us to worry or obsess about what lies ahead.

Keeping watch means preparing both for a future on this earth and for our future in the world to come. It means preparing for our children's future in this world—saving money for their studies and teaching them skills and values they will need to succeed. It also means preparing them for that day when their life on this earth comes to an end and they meet their Savior face to face. Most important, it means trusting that whatever happens, the future is always in God's reliable hands. As Christians, we have nothing to fear, in this world or the next.

Merciful God,
grant me the foresight
and
wisdom
to help my family prepare for
both of our futures—
on this earth
and
in heaven.
In Jesus' name.
Amen.

The Most Important "Job" in the World

Genesis 18:1–15; Luke 1:26–38

In the middle of the desert, Abraham and Sarah entertained three strangers. These strangers turned out to be angels—announcing the good news that in their old age, Abraham and Sarah would become parents to a son (Genesis 18). In Galilee, the angel Gabriel appeared to the virgin Mary and proclaimed that she would conceive by the Holy Spirit and give birth to "the Son of God" (Luke 1:35).

We remember well the day we learned we would become parents for the first time. We experienced great joy. We even danced and sang a little. There were no angels, however, and no great heavenly drama. Perhaps it was the same for you. You learned about your new calling without the benefit of angel visitors.

God called Abraham and Sarah, Mary, and many others to be parents. Without all the bells and whistles, God also called you. A lack of drama does not make your role as a parent any less significant. Parenting is *always* a calling, a vocation.

For Christians, a vocation is the work God asks us to do every day. Parenting is not simply a job or a task or a chore. It is much more. God calls women and men to take on the vocation of caring for the smallest people in creation.

Since becoming parents, we have noticed how other people often undervalue the vocation of parenting. A friend of ours reports that she often feels invisible at social gatherings. "Because I stay home to care for my small children, people sometimes think I don't do anything. They certainly don't give me credit for having a brain."

God views parenting differently. God has cared enough about parenting throughout the centuries to choose specific people like Abraham, Sarah, and Mary to become fathers and mothers. In many ways, God has made it clear that parenting is the most important "job" in the world.

What does it mean for parenting to be our vocation? It means, more than anything, that we participate in the lives of our children. We listen to them. We pay attention to their actions. We spend time with them. We choose to be present with them physically, emotionally, and spiritually. Mary provides a good example. She was present throughout Jesus' ministry on earth and as He was dying on the cross (see John 19:25). Mary remained by Jesus' side even after His closest disciples had abandoned Him.

Being a parent also means that we take seriously the vows we made on the day our children were baptized. We bring them to church. We read the Bible with them. We teach them the Creeds, the Lord's Prayer, and the Ten Commandments. Through it all, we remind them that in the midst of everything life brings us, we depend on our Lord and Savior, Jesus Christ for our salvation.

Sound daunting? Yes, it does. And it should. Parenting *is* the *most important job in the world*. But remember—when God calls us to do something, God also gives us the skills and endurance to get the job done. Whenever we feel overwhelmed, we draw inspiration from the angel Gabriel's final words to Mary when he announced our Savior's impending birth: "For nothing is impossible with God" (Luke 1:37).

Prayer idea:

> Throughout the day,
> as you care for your children,
> stop several times and say,
> "God has called me to this task."
> Then thank God for giving you the skills
> and the strength necessary to complete it.

Cuddle Time

We have a new addition to our bedtime ritual. We call it "cuddle time." Besides reading a story and saying our prayers, one of us spends a few moments each night sitting next to Sam in a big comfy chair. We talk about how our day has been. We look forward to the coming morning, making a list of activities we want to do. We speak kind words to each other, such as "Sam, I'm so proud of how you shared with your friend Anya today." And, of course, we cuddle. Before we send Sam off to bed, we sing a song and thank God for our many blessings.

"Cuddle time" enables us to reconnect with Sam each night, no matter what the day has been like. Parenting has its difficult moments. In the heat of life's daily activities, we can easily forget what is most important—that we love our child, that this little one is a gift to us from God, that God has trusted us to raise Sam to grow in faith and love toward his Savior. "Cuddle time" brings life's big picture back into focus.

"Cuddle time" with Sam also reminds us that we need to make room in our schedules for "cuddle time" with God. We often become so involved in our daily commitments we forget what is most important—that God loves us and makes us His own. We lose sight of the fact that our lives are a gift from God, that God is there to help us grow in faith and love toward our Savior.

If we want our relationships to be rich and healthy, we need to give them our time and attention. Before we began to have "cuddle time" with Sam each night, we often forgot how important it was to assure Sam of our love for him. Our relationship with our son has improved since we added our evening ritual. We never have the option of skipping because Sam, with the perfect memory, reminds us each evening when it's time to cuddle.

Our relationship with God is no different from our earthly relationships. To flourish, our relationship with God needs our time and attention. We need daily "cuddle time" with God. We cannot simply go to church once a week and expect that will be enough to sustain a healthy relationship with God. Our covenant relationship with God is deepened through daily moments of prayer and study, time to strengthen our bond and to communicate our deepest needs.

The Gospels tells us that many times during His ministry on earth, Jesus went off to solitary places to connect with our heavenly Father. At the garden of Gethsemane, just hours before His arrest and crucifixion, Jesus fell to the ground and prayed *"Abba,* Father" (Mark 14:36). Jesus stayed connected with the One from whom He came and to whom He would return.

Of course, God will continue to love us even if we neglect our relationship with Him. It's not for God's benefit that we need to spend time with Him—it's for our own. When our schedules become overwhelming and we fail to take time to read the Bible (God's Words of love to us) or open our hearts to our gracious Savior, we can quickly forget how much God loves us. We pray that the Holy Spirit works through this book of devotions and helps you cultivate your relationship with God through Jesus Christ. We pray that Christ's love will nourish and comfort you as you continue the blessed journey of parenting.

God of my past,
present, and future,
thank You for the moments
we have spent together as I have read this book.
Today and in the future,
encourage me to always keep You first in my life.
In Jesus' name.
Amen.

Timeouts
with

God